Reader Reviews from

Reyna's conveyance of her fa[...] [...] [...]s
connected with me. The commentary is thought-provoking and inspirational
for people from all walks of life. Once you read "The Tape Recorder," you
will want to share it.
—Mindy Burden, FL

I think your dad's words and stories will change people.
—Mary McCartney, NC

I offer many hallelujahs for "The Tape Recorder" and Reyna's efforts to
spread the timeless, precious testimony of Jesus Christ's power in the life of
Rianco Rivera. Reyna undoubtedly fulfills part of her heavenly destiny as she
chronicles her father's simple and powerful child-like faith seasoned with her
genuine, heartfelt reflections the reader can immediately apply to life. Having
read this book, I join my voice with Rianco's: "The Lord is good! Hallelujah!
Thank you, Jesus!"
—Jesse Smith, author of Restoring Christian Modesty: God's Perfect Will
For Your Outward Appearance

The Tape Recorder is a beautiful reflection of a daughter's devotion to
keeping her late father's stories alive. The author is thoughtful in retelling
the miraculous events that took place in her father's lifetime. Her re-creation
transports you to the tree under which her father sat with his tape recorder.
Her descriptions paint a picture so clear, it feels as though you had taken
part in these miracles. You won't be able to put this book down. These
heartwarming stories will give you something to believe in.
—Sarah W., OH

Initially, I was truly lost for words. As an experienced songwriter I understand
how difficult it can be to bare your soul for the world to see. Rianco Rivera
did just that when he recorded and documented his journey from a life of
turbulence and substance abuse to that of an avid follower of Jesus Christ.
Reyna Rivera maintained the integrity of her father's story when she wrote
this manuscript. Her ability and desire to keep the story as raw and honest as
the original recording speaks to her character as a writer and certainly causes
her to bare her own soul. Not only did I find this journey incredibly moving

but it drew emotions and tears that I never anticipated. I was so drawn to this amazing story that I had to read it straight through without a break!!!!
—T.W. Crossen, Artist's Music Guild Songwriter of The Year 2018

The Tape Recorder captured my attention from the moment I began reading as it dealt with experiences of real people who worked hard to make a living in 1940's to present day. The author's father used to live for himself and then came to know Jesus as his Savior. He was forever changed as were the people in his prayer life. I enjoyed every page and was amazed how the recording her father made became a book at the hands of his daughter.
—Ps.Samuel Vasquez, Senior Pastor Iglesia Evangelica Amigos, Agujita, Coahuila, Mexico. President of the Pastors Alliance of the State of Coahuila, Mexico

The Tape Recorder captures the grace of God with a child-like innocence and shows what God expects blind faith to look like. Like a true Believer, Rianco does not underestimate his own power of prayer.

His daughter skillfully narrated how her father acted in pure honest faith, capturing his plain and dead-honest voice while recording the knowledge he had. This alone made the book refreshing to read.

What I have been able to own from reading this book is three-fold: the power of true faith; the wonder of true love; and the glory of hope. Ultimately, faith, love and hope are what conquers, and is all that is important. That is enough to remain.
—Ps. Frederick Paul Pickering, Johannesburg, South Africa

The Tape Recorder

Adapted and Retold from a Tape
Recording by Rianco Rivera

Reyna Rivera

Reyna Rivera

ISBN: 978-1-4834-2275-6 (sc)
ISBN: 978-1-4834-2414-9 (e)

Library of Congress Control Number: 2019909990

Interior Image Credit: Reyna Rivera

Scripture quotations marked NLV are taken from the New Life Version, copyright © 1969 and 2003. Used by permission of Barbour Publishing, Inc., Uhrichsville, Ohio 44683. All rights reserved.

Scripture quotations marked (AMP) are taken from the Amplified Bible, Copyright © 2015 by The Lockman Foundation. Used by permission.

Lulu Publishing Services rev. date: 09/25/2019

To honor my parents, Rianco and Renata.
They are loved and missed beyond all measure.

If I am gonna tell you things that have happened to me,
things that I have asked the Lord to do for me, then I
want to tell you the story from the beginning.

—Rianco Rivera

CONTENTS

AUTHOR'S NOTE

In order to protect the privacy of family members both deceased and living, I have changed the names, dates, and locations included in this book. The purity of our family legacy has been altered, but I have recalled the stories in such a manner as to respect and honor the memory of my father's factual stories as he recorded them.

While you read this narrative, it is important to note that this manuscript includes quotes from my father, who had a strong accent. I have included his exact words so you can hear his voice. He was born in 1925, was raised in Texas, spoke Spanish, and had an eighth-grade education. In 1951, my parents moved our growing family north to southern Ohio, and he adapted by becoming bilingual, but he never lost his strong Tex-Mex accent.

PREFACE

On the day of my father's funeral in 2015, a niece gave me a gift: a cassette tape Dad had recorded to chronicle his Christian walk. None of his nine now-orphaned adult offspring had known it existed. In it, he requested that the collection of powerful, inspirational testimonies be published and disseminated so others could hear how God undeniably had used his grateful heart and prayers of faith to change the lives of family members and strangers for fifty-seven years.

I transcribed the audio recordings and compiled them into this format so I could retell each sound bite. New details emerged as a result of discussions with family members and online research. I incorporated his personal dialogue in his Tex-Mex broken English so the reader could hear his voice. As a result of my efforts to share this collection in a manner that honors his memory, it was impossible not to add my own reflections of personal growth.

The task came full circle. Dad recorded his testimonies to show how God had directed him as an instrument of prayer to impact lives, and he hoped that somehow, they would be published.

As I transcribed the audio and worked on this manuscript, the process impacted my life as well. I can only wonder how many more lives will be changed. Dad said, "I didn't heal the people. God healed the people. I just prayed for the people."

Before Dad undertook the task of recording his Christian testimonies, as requested by a church friend, he wanted to pray and reflect on which stories he would include in this seemingly insurmountable project. As his daughter, I have no proof that he ever had undertaken such a task prior to his recording the single cassette tape. I believe prayer was the avenue he would have taken in order to form a comfortable mind-set and assure himself that he would be producing the recording for the right reason—to glorify the Lord. He felt strongly that an apology to his friend was in order, as he had not begun the recording project in a timely manner. She had empowered him by providing the tape recorder and cassettes and encouraged him with words of inspiration. After he made the apology, he felt he could finally press the Record button on the donated tape recorder with a clear conscience.

ACKNOWLEDGMENTS

With a grateful heart, I thank Jesus Christ for providing everything I needed at just the right time to fulfill my dad's wish to have his story published and in the hands of people whose lives will be impacted by his cassette recordings. Many thanks to my niece who presented me with the original cassette tape Dad recorded. She had received it from her mother, who, along with a friend, had encouraged Dad to share his personal testimonies for publication. It is their wish to remain anonymous and, in doing so, give all the glory to Jesus Christ as they help to further advance the message of salvation.

Without the encouragement, support, and input of my siblings as I took the initiative to pursue Dad's voiced desire to "somehow, someway" have his Christian testimonies "written in a book," this project would not have happened. I am grateful to my three children, who listened to me retell or read the first draft of the first story I transcribed and encouraged me to continue the monumental task. Without a doubt, Gwen was my first editor and sounding board; she listened, read, and scrutinized all the minutia involved in putting each chapter onto paper during our long walks along the lake trail even though she had begun her journey of being diagnosed with the early stages of Lewy body disease. I admire her strength, tenacity, editing skills, and sense of humor and am forever thankful.

Two uncles, nieces, nephews, countless cousins, and many friends provided details that enriched the content of this project. My parents, who were avid followers of Jesus Christ's teachings, laid the building blocks that formed our characters as children. We memorized the Ten Commandments, which provided a moral compass to grow by. Mom taught us that just because we were poor did not mean we had to appear unkempt. Every tortilla I turned on the comal, each meal I ate of homemade buttered biscuits, and even every meal I didn't eat because I didn't like the smell of menudo was a life lesson that fertilized and nurtured my soul. Dad faithfully traveled to work each day, regardless of the road conditions, which were especially treacherous during the winter, in order to provide for his growing family, enduring the constant and daily pain in his right knee. Our parents kept our family together as they hovered over their brood, standing beside us—through the good and bad decisions we made—as we spread our wings, and one day each of us left the nest, not necessarily in the order in which we had arrived. Now each of us has the wisdom to tell our own grown children, nieces and nephews, and grandchildren that there is no parenting manual and that we can only make decisions based on the information we have at any given moment. Yes, Dad was right: troubles come to us, and we have our ingrained faith to remind us we are never alone, and that alone will be enough to see us through.

Thanks to Bill and Kathy for suggesting that I consider Lulu Press for my self-publishing project; Caroline for her sleuth skills in tracking down a tape recorder; Rosina, Angelo, Armin, and Larry for their photography skills; Bruce and Jeremy for their help in the technical transcription of the original cassette recording; Barbara, Mary, Debbie, Portia, Tina, Sarah, Rosina, Anne, Mindy and the Cantu's for reading various chapters; and Tracy for her gentle reminder to "live life to **live** it."

Last of all, I wish to acknowledge my husband, who tolerated the time I spent at the computer keyboard. I knew all along that he did not want to read the manuscript until the last word had been entered. As a result, it was easy for him to suggest the title of my dad's book, which I proudly added with the push of my fingers just like Dad had pushed the buttons on the tape recorder.

INTRODUCTION

In my dad's younger days, he led a lifestyle that included substance abuse and the chaos it created, including domestic violence. After he began to live a Christian life, he became a changed man who had faith that inspired him to pray with and for others. The results of his prayers are indisputable.

A friend heard Dad give accounts of how his grateful heart had led him to obey the guidance of the Holy Spirit. Through intercessory prayer, he asked God to intervene in the lives of others. He made his prayer requests in faith. God found favor with his prayer requests, and lives were forever changed.

Fourteen of those true short stories have been compiled in this book. The chapter "Right Time, Right Place" tells of how his prayer for a sick man was answered, though with delayed healing, and there was a surprise element to his obedience. Dad's faith in the promises of God was strong enough to move mountains, as illustrated in "Just Enough Time," which tells of the time he requested prayers for safe travel prior to a road trip, and there was no time to pray at the critical moment of need. Dad believed that you and I could ask anything in the name of Jesus, and it would be given. In fact, it was his firm belief that Jesus could do greater things than we could even think of asking. "Reyna Fall Down" tells of the time my chest was crushed by a car Dad had been driving. Dad did the only thing he knew how to do: he prayed. Right then and there, he humbled himself and guided his family to kneel and pray in a puddle of mud. "Her Name Is Renata" recalls how Mom did not survive the complications of childbirth, but then a prayer of faith brought her back to life immediately.

Dad liked to say, "If you obey Him, He can come through for you." I think that in his broken English, he was indicating that the Lord will provide a way for your prayers to be answered if it is His will and if He will be glorified. For example, He provided everything Dad needed to record these amazing true stories and then—somehow, someway—provided the means for you to read the stories of this simple, humble, faithful servant of the Lord.

CHAPTER 1

You Can Hear a Little Birdie Singing

D ad describes how he was inspired to record his Christian testimonies as he sits outside the family home, under a big shade tree that is home to birds and other wildlife in the area. As I listened to the recordings, I could hear the birds singing in the background, and the session ends with Dad singing as well.

Dad begins recording as he remembers the details of 1951, when he brought his young family—his wife of four years and three children—from Texas to Ohio in the back of a migrant work truck. My grandparents loved my dad but also hoped that by forcing him to move away from the environment that had fueled his alcoholism, marijuana use, and other habits that were deemed unsavory during the time, he would turn his life around for the better. The decision my grandparents made reminds me of what we call a "tough-love move."

During that time of Dad's life, he tells us, he was "a mean man." He didn't trust anyone when it came to them advising him how to live his life. I have heard stories about his bad temper, which he demonstrated in public places, and the domestic abuse that followed. I am sure it was hard for him to put that part of his life into words. He describes himself with these words: "I used to live for the world. I was hardened like a rock. My heart was like a rock."

I think it is important to give you a snapshot of the national economy at the time. To do that, I accessed data from the 1940 Federal United States

Census,[1] which is the latest census report released to the public. It reveals a few details that helped me understand his home life, the world political climate, and the national economy.

The Rivera household included nine children living in the home Grandpa owned. He was employed as a deliveryman, and he had worked fifty-two weeks of the previous year, earning under $1,000. We don't know if the two oldest sons, who were employed as farm laborers, were expected to contribute money from their pay to help make ends meet within the family home. The data shows that two of his older brothers were earning ten dollars a week.

Dad had an eighth-grade education. He had a job harvesting crops under the hot Texas sun. His estimated income in 1940, as a fifteen-year-old, was five dollars per week, and he had worked the previous year for a duration of thirty weeks. Certainly, he had funds to support his unhealthy lifestyle.

According to the website Biography.com, World War II occurred from 1939 to 1945, and the national economy was beginning to recover when Harry S. Truman was sworn into office in 1945 as the thirty-third president of the United States, taking office because of the untimely death of Franklin Delano Roosevelt. The federal minimum wage was four dollars an hour, gasoline was twenty-one cents a gallon, milk was sixty-seven cents a gallon, and the price of a movie ticket would set you back fifty-five cents.[2]

By 1950, Grandpa Rivera had a crisis at home. Grandma's health had begun to deteriorate. A teenage son—who was possibly bipolar, according to a family member—threatened a family member with a kitchen knife. After that incident, my grandparents feared for their own safety around their son, which prompted them to seek more intense medical attention.

There were more difficult decisions for my grandparents to make because of economic conditions and the reality of supporting a large family. The family gathered information, weighed their options, and came

---

[1] "United States Census, 1940," database with images, FamilySearch, citing Sixteenth Census of the United States, Records of the Bureau of the Census, 1790–2017, Washington, DC, National Archives and Records Administration, 2012, accessed January 30, 2019, https://FamilySearch.org.

[2] "Harry S. Truman Biography," accessed March 13, 2019, www.biography.com/people/harry-s-truman-9511121.

to the conclusion that they would encourage the four oldest adult offspring to relocate their young families to the northern state of Ohio, where other local friends had found jobs. They would still have five children near or at home to help with Grandma's deteriorating health issues. In hindsight, it's clear they made a good decision, as all four of the young families who left Texas found viable employment opportunities and, as a result, raised their own families in the North and never returned to live in their home state of Texas.

When my parents got married in 1947, Dad continued his bad habits, which were already well established. By 1951, when they relocated to Ohio, Mom was battling to keep herself and her young family housed, fed, and safe from Dad's abusive nature. Perhaps her hopes of a fresh start in a new environment vanished. I don't have any memories of her revealing the abuse and despair she must have endured during her early marriage.

When talking about those first years in Ohio, from 1951 to 1958, before Dad became a Christian, he talks about feeling lost, but he didn't change his day-to-day routine. He worked menial-labor jobs and supplemented his income by tending crops or harvesting them to make ends meet. He was also still exhibiting bad habits associated with substances.

As I worked through the process of writing this manuscript, I got a gentle reminder and a glimmer of hope when I heard Dad say, "All these troubles that come to us, they come because we serve the Lord. But we are in good hands because Jesus is on our side." Like my father, I believe that one day God will make us aware of why He allows troubles to enter our lives.

Dad's heart was softened when he finally surrendered his life to Jesus Christ in 1958. He tells us, "When Jesus saved my soul, He gave me a tender heart; I had a loving heart for people. And now I live for Him. Jesus has come through for me. I have prayed for people many times. I have prayed for sick people, and they were healed." The Lord provided a way for his prayers to be answered.

I was nearly a seven-year-old the day my father gave his life to Christ. I have no memory of him being drunk; foul-mouthed; or verbally, emotionally, or physically abusive. I do remember that prior to his Christian life, he and my uncle would buy cases of beer and use them as outdoor seats on hot summer nights as we played outdoors, catching fireflies or playing hide-and-seek, with cousins. I also recall finding divorce papers

Mom had hidden, but I didn't know what implications they held until I wrote this manuscript.

My dad stopped "living for the world," as he describes it. He believed that if he did his best to live for Jesus, he would never be left alone or forsaken. Dad believed that Jesus wanted people to "grow closer to Him," which, according to his beliefs, could be achieved through obedience, faith, and prayer.

Dad begins this tape portion of his recording session with these words: "And tonight, as I begin to record these stories, I pray because I want to know that I am doing this for the right reason. But I haven't made time until today to begin talking into this recorder." His friends intended to transcribe the stories for Dad so they could be shared with others, but the mechanics of transcribing his broken English derailed their best-laid plans. Therefore, the project lay dormant in their hands until after his death, at which time the cassette tape Dad had given them to transcribe was presented to me.

I have felt the same feelings he talks about while he ponders the task of recording his stories. When he was asked to record his testimonies, he had to be talked into the project, it seems. I heard the nervousness in his voice as I listened to the beginning of the one-sided dialogue of "Dad Gets a Message from God." It was evident he had trouble learning how to work the machine. Perhaps he wondered if he would remember which button he needed to press for each function or how to work out the timing sequence of speaking into the microphone, which is obvious, because some of the audio portion is missing.

He talks about not "[making] time until today to begin talking into this recorder." I, too, put the project aside several times before this manuscript took its present form. I got the cassette recording on the day of Dad's funeral in January 2015. I typed the manuscript in a timely manner but then set the project aside because I didn't have direction or a purpose. I had the cassette transferred onto CD and then finally onto a thumb drive two years later. Still, there was no apparent reason or direction for a finished project. It wasn't until I was recording family genealogy that the project began to take form and substance in my mind.

I waited for feedback from my siblings and other family members who offered their support and contributions to this body of work. As I undertook this project, I didn't have a scope and sequence or know the final outcome of the project. I didn't feel like an author, as the recordings are in my dad's voice. I took special care to keep his originality and intention as pure as the day he pushed Record. Even though the cassette tape was in my hands, I didn't feel sole ownership of the stories. I felt strongly that even though the recording was given to me that frigid day we buried Dad, all nine of his offspring are the stewards of this collection, and soon the stories will be owned—and stored as treasures—in the hearts of our children and grandchildren. Ultimately, only God knows the reason for this labor of love. Just like Dad, I pray because I want to know that I am doing this for the right reason.

As I transcribed Dad's words for you in these fourteen stories, I discovered that my thoughts mimic his. I want to know that every word I put onto paper has been placed within this manuscript for the right reason. God provided me with everything I needed at the right time to accomplish this task. He did not leave me alone. He did not forsake me. I firmly believe that no word I have included will return void. I noticed that Dad did not use exact scripture quotations as he recorded his stories; however, the inferences are there.

This biblical passage is clearly applicable: "So will My word be which goes out of My mouth; It will not return to Me void [useless, without result], Without accomplishing what I desire, And without succeeding in the matter for which I sent it." (Isaiah 55:11 AMP)

I interpret that quote to mean that while I don't know which chapter, word, phrase, or quote will reach the heart of a particular reader, with a moral certainty, I do know the project is in God's hands. Like my dad, I am not well versed in providing biblical quotes, but a nephew agreed to contribute appropriate scripture references, which you will find at the end of each chapter.

To conclude this chapter, I have included part of Dad's text because I realize I cannot change a single word that this simple man left for you to read. He said it best. It is my belief that the following message will not fail to resonate in someone's heart:

> If you are listening to my testimony on the tape recorder, you can hear the little birdie singing, because I am sitting beside a birdhouse. All the little birdies come to the

birdhouse, and they begin singing songs. And I praise the Lord for that!

And tonight, I just want to ask that somehow, somewhere, if you are not saved today, why don't you make up your mind to give your heart to Jesus? Surrender to Jesus. It don' gonna cost you nothing. It's just like … if you want to get saved and you are by yourself, you can talk to Jesus, just like everybody else does. And Jesus can touch you and save your soul. In the name of Jesus!

And sometimes I say to myself, "If I am gonna serve the Lord, I wanna serve Him with all my heart." And tonight, I am gonna keep talking into this recorder so that people can know that if they are not saved, they *got* to be saved. They have to try the best they can to get closer to Jesus and be saved so that they can be ready. He is coming soon!

Jesus promised us that He would never leave us alone. When He comes back, He is going to come back through the clouds. He is gonna pick up the Christians that are still living, and we're gonna meet him in the air! Oh, hallelujah!

Sometimes I like to sing a little song with a chorus that says,

I know the Lord will make a way for me.
If I live a holy life,
Shun the wrong, and do the right,
I know the Lord will make a way for me.

The song he sings is "I Know the Lord Will Make a Way for Me" by Paul Epps. Dad closes this recording session with his classic, "Hallelujah! Thank You, Jesus! He saved my soul! Hallelujah!"

So, My Word which goes from My mouth will not return to Me empty. It will do what I want it to do, and will carry out My plan well. **Isaiah (55:11 NLV)**

CHAPTER 2

Dad Gets a Message from God

When a family friend felt compelled to deliver a message to my father, he rejected it. This account describes the progression of how God called Dad to leave a substance-fueled life behind and follow the call of Jesus Christ.

Dad grew up in a Catholic family, and they were active at their local church. As youngsters, Dad and a friend stole their first drinks of alcohol from the sacristy while volunteering as altar boys. By the time Dad was sixteen years old, by his own admission, he was drinking so much that he had reached an alcoholic state.

The Lord spoke to him through Odilia, a family friend, for the first time when he was eighteen years old. She arrived at Grandpa and Grandma's family home to speak to him on a Saturday morning while he was eating breakfast.

She said, "Rianco, I have a message from God that I need you to hear. The Lord wants to save your soul. You better make up your mind today. Because tomorrow it might be too late. Won't you let me pray with you?"

He agreed to let her pray and read scriptures from the Bible for him. The visit that day began during breakfast but didn't end until four o'clock that afternoon. That day, the Lord guided Odilia to begin laying a foundation in his heart by telling him about Christ's love for all mankind, including him, even though he was an *alcoholico*, as he would say.

As the extended visit and conversation came to a close, he avoided making a decision to live for Christ, and in his broken English, he explained to her, "I don' have time for the stuff of the Bible. I never pay attention

7

to it. I know that the Lord don' love me, 'cause I don' make time to live for Him."

At the close of her visit, he informed her that he was going to continue drinking and that he could go anywhere anytime and do anything he wanted. To counteract his bad habits, as a Catholic, he tells us, he felt that all he had to do was go to confession after he did bad things, and then he could repeat any of his sins and confess again. The cycle of visiting the confessional booth was well practiced, and the path to that door was well worn.

Later that night, it was evident the Lord had His hand on Dad, even though he had rejected His message of salvation, which Odilia had obediently delivered earlier that day. While at a local beer joint, he became involved in a bar fight. He thought he was a tough guy and could handle himself, as he was always armed with a razor blade for protection. As it turned out, he needed the Lord's protection that night and not the protection of a razor blade or gun.

The fight eventually spilled onto the street. His body was badly beaten. On the tape recording, he claimed he couldn't remember many details about the reason for the altercation. He did recall being kneed in the stomach, punched, and kicked, and he also suffered a deep cut at the back of his head. Rodolfo, a classmate, witnessed the incident; recognized the person inflicting the beating; and decided to run home to get his own weapon of choice so he could protect Dad and himself if need be.

When Rodolfo returned, he saw that Dad had been dragged to the nearby railroad tracks, where people were often intentionally dumped onto the tracks. In relocating Dad's beaten body, his attackers hoped a passing train would complicate any investigation and destroy evidence of their involvement. Rodolfo knew that a local train would be on those tracks at four o'clock in the morning, and if he didn't intervene, Dad more than likely would die there. Local authorities would be led to believe the fatal injuries of the mutilated body found at the site indicated that the victim had died while attempting to cross the train tracks in a drunken stupor.

As the situation escalated, Rodolfo felt compelled to pull his .45-caliber handgun out of his pocket and threaten the man with it in order to stop the beating. By the grace of God, that friend saved Dad from being run over by a train that night.

But Dad continued to harden his heart to the things of the Lord. Even after that severe beating, he did not change his lifestyle.

As time passed, he met his future wife, Renata, who was a Christian, and his bad habits subsided a bit. Even though he had a religious upbringing, he claims he didn't know anything about the Bible. Still, the Lord began to change his heart. When Mom was twenty-two years old and Dad was twenty-one, they married, and children began to arrive at the Rivera household.

Dad still went out drinking and often did not come back until the next day. As a new bride, Mom would get upset with him, as it seemed his drinking habits worsened. Their new marriage was in trouble. Even so, nobody was going to tell him to change his bad habits, not even a new bride pleading with him to change his ways for the sake of his growing family.

Still, the Lord continued to have his protecting hand on him and his family at all times. If it were not for Him, Dad believes, he would not have been alive to record these stories.

I remember hearing that Dad, Mom, and their three children traveled north to Ohio aboard a migrant worker's farm truck. Dad called it the *tomatero* truck. As the years passed, that same migrant family who had provided his family with transportation from Texas to Ohio would stop by our house in southern Ohio for visits during the summer, tomato-picking season. Over the years, I began to look forward to their visits because their older kids would share their copies of the newest *Archie and Veronica* comic books with us. We were delighted when they would leave a stack of comic books for us to read, and then we would give them back when they stopped again en route to the next migrant camp. I now realize their truck served as a traveling library of the times.

Dad wasn't interested in harvesting cotton or tomatoes during the summers under the hot sunshine. He looked for other work and got a job, as did my uncle, working at Oscar's Grain and Feed, which was located in the little town where our family lived in migrant housing. According to a first cousin, other family members who had migrated north for the chance to live a life better than picking cotton or tomatoes in the crop fields got their starts there as well. I was the first of six children born in Ohio.

Dad continued to drink heavily and carry a switchblade, he was still involved with substances, and domestic violence thrived within our modest and not-so-private accommodations. He recounts that the police were trying to find him one night after he had difficulty controlling his drinking and drug problem and, subsequently, came home and was physically abusive to Mom. Someone living within the migrant compound—more than likely a relative—called the police to report the incident, which prompted him to pack up his family and leave the compound in the middle of the night to escape apprehension by the authorities.

When he evaded the police that night, he felt his actions were clever, as he uses the words *pretty smart* to describe his decision to leave the compound under the cover of darkness. I cannot explain his use or meaning of the words *pretty smart*. As I discussed this incident with relatives and compared Dad's cassette tape, it was obvious he avoided talking about the violence he had inflicted on his young wife, which, more than likely, my older siblings witnessed as youngsters.

Eventually, our parents set up permanent housekeeping in a small town, in a home that our oldest brother now owns and occupies. The move to a new town didn't help Dad control his bad habits, and his marriage was in turmoil. I found divorce papers that someone had placed on the top shelf of Mom's blue kitchen cabinet one day, along with a pack of cigarettes. I never saw the document or cigarettes again after having whispered conversations with my siblings. I assume that after his *Come-to-Jesus* moment, Dad carried the burden of his wrongdoings and trusted the Lord for forgiveness. It is my sincere hope that my parents discussed the trauma Mom had suffered at Dad's hands and worked out their feelings with the help of a spiritual adviser during their many decades of marriage.

My brothers tell stories about how serious Dad's involvement with alcohol and drugs had gotten. In order to hide his drinking and drug problem, Dad would take my two oldest brothers downtown to watch Saturday matinees. He'd give them enough money for the movie, popcorn, and a beverage. Then he would walk across the street to the bar at the Line Hotel and begin drinking. My brothers would watch the movie several times before Dad finally walked—or stumbled—back across the street to pick them up. Of course, that was not pleasant for my brothers, and neither was the car ride home. The road leading home was straight, with one left-hand turn. My brother tells me that sometimes the turn would be navigated on two wheels instead of four.

During those early years in Ohio, Mom would take us to church. She would make Dad attend services on Mother's Day, Christmas, and Easter, even if he had been drinking. After church, Dad would accuse Mom of talking to the preacher about his alcohol use behind his back, and on the cassette tape, he admits to accusingly confronting her by asking, "Why did you talk to the preacher about it?" I can't imagine the beating that ensued. I never heard Mom talk about being a battered housewife. Whatever she suffered, she never uttered a word, nor did I ever suspect the trauma she endured during those early years of marriage, when Dad, as he says, "lived for the world." She must have been a strong woman.

I found no hint of an explanation on the tape recording that provides insight into what was happening to Dad's heart while he listened in church prior to his transformation, when he "lived for the world." I assume the preacher's sermons hit close to home deep within his guilt-ridden heart. God was still in control, and the seeds Odilia had planted when he was eighteen years old had already begun to sprout. Additionally, God fortified those seeds through the healing experience Dad witnessed of his infant daughter, which is presented in the next chapter.

On Saturday, June 14, 1958, I was in the car with Mom and all my siblings while Ruben, a family friend, went into the local beer joint at the Line Hotel to talk to Dad. It is safe to assume the male friend also delivered a message from God to Dad. When they came out of the bar, Dad was a changed man. He bought each of us children and Mom an ice cream cone, and he was extremely happy. I did not know the significance of the events that had unfolded while they were inside the establishment. At the time, the only thing important to me was that it was indeed a special day because I didn't have to share an ice cream cone with a sister or a brother.

When he walked out of the Line Hotel bar, Dad says, he felt as if he were in a trance. He was crying and could not speak. He knew he had heard the voice of God. Dad says he heard the voice of the Lord speak to him that day while he was in the beer joint. God said, **"Get out of here. You don't belong here!"**

He goes on to tell us that after he heard the voice of God tell him to get out of the beer joint that Saturday afternoon, he didn't drink anymore.

11

He didn't swear anymore. He didn't do anything bad anymore. His life had been changed. He wanted to be nice to his family, and, he confesses, it was easy to be nice to other people as well. The Lord had given him a big family whom he loved and needed to care and provide for. It was then that he realized it was bad for him to be a *drunker*, as Dad called himself.

However, two weeks later, on Saturday, June 28, 1958, God's plan for Dad's life began to unfold in an even bigger way. Dad took his big family to a little church where Spanish people were gathering for worship services. When the minister, Reverend Ray, invited attendees to step forward for prayer during the altar call to publicly confess their sins to Jesus, Dad was in the middle of a group of eighteen people who gave their lives to Christ that night.

I have memories of that night. As we climbed the steep steps up to the entrance of the church, I could hear the sounds of guitars, pianos, drums, and various other musical instruments being tuned. The parking lot was crowded, and there was standing room only inside the sanctuary. People shared hymnals printed in Spanish, which I was unable to read, but I could understand the songs, as Mom and Dad spoke both their native language and English at home.

I didn't know what was happening during the altar call, but I did know that my dad walked forward to the front of the church among that group of people. There was loud singing, along with prayers and joyous cries of happiness. Sweet voices sang hymns and filled the atmosphere, seeming to float toward the rafters and through the roof, heaven bound. I witnessed people in a public setting humble themselves before Christ to confess their sins and, in return, be blessed by the Lord Almighty, Jesus Christ.

Dad tells us that it was eleven-thirty that night when he got back onto his feet after kneeling at the altar for what seemed like hours to him. He had confessed his sins and accepted Jesus as his personal Savior.

"I felt I was walking on air, because the Lord had cleaned me! He had made me whole! He had saved my soul!" Dad exclaims.

Dad believed his life had unfolded according to God's perfect plan.

He tells us, "The story of my life is so long that I could continue talking all day and all night."

My father, Rianco, recorded these stories while sitting under a shade tree at the family home four years after Mom passed on to Glory, did his best to share what it was like to have lived a Christian life. The Lord put all of these stories on his heart, and I am honored to be the instrument God assigned to bring the stories to you.

Dad again closes his session with enthusiastic praises: "In the name of Jesus! Hallelujah! Amen."

> *But you are a chosen group of people. You are the King's religious leaders. You are a holy nation. You belong to God. He has done this for you so you can tell others how God has called you out of darkness into His great light.* (**1 Peter 2:9 NLV**)

CHAPTER 3

Ramona

This is a simple anecdote of God's plan for prayer, faith, healing, and the softening of a hardened heart through the life of Dad's infant daughter. Dad felt that God used this experience as a building block of faith, prior to his spiritual conversion. My sister is now in her sixties and remembers Dad sharing this testimony during church services about her healing.

Baby number five had arrived in the Rivera family, and she was given a name that began with the letter *R*, just as all the other children had been. Her given name was Ramona. She was born in Ohio, so I can assume she was born at Riverton Hospital, where I, too, was born.

I bring that up to remind you that Dad packed up the family one night and fled the migrant compound in the small town where we had been living, because someone had reported his abusive nature toward Mom to the authorities. That night, he moved our family out of that town and headed west, eventually establishing the family homestead in an even smaller village.

Dad must have wondered how to tell this accounting truthfully yet avoid including unpleasant details that would have shed light on his violent nature as a substance abuser. I make that assumption because he seems distracted while speaking into the tape recorder, as indicated by the way he stops and starts the machine. He explains that he felt he needed to take more time to think about how to describe the long and short of it. He doesn't mention the night he fled town with the family. I assume he wanted to avoid bringing up painful memories and the guilt associated with his negative lifestyle.

Shortly after her birth, Ramona became ill. My parents sought medical attention for the infant, and the attending physician prescribed medication but cautioned them by saying he didn't know if the medicine would help. He hoped the dosage would enable her to live through the night.

As it happened, by eleven o'clock that night, baby Ramona was having difficulty breathing, and death seemed imminent. Mom didn't know whom to turn to for help. Remembering that she had the telephone number for the pastor of the local church, where she had faithfully begun taking her five children to attend worship services, out of desperation, she pleaded with Dad to call the pastor and request that he come to the house to pray for the baby.

There was no telephone in our home, so he drove to a restaurant that was still open, where there was access to a phone. Even though it was late, the minister's wife answered the telephone, and she informed Dad that she would send her husband to the house to offer a prayer as soon as he got home. At one-thirty in the morning, the minister arrived to pray for the infant, anointed her head with oil, and then offered his prayer for healing to heaven. Mom believed in the power of prayer because she was a believer. Dad was a nonbeliever at the time, but this day, he had a front-row seat to witness the power of God and what He was able and willing to do in the lives of his obedient, faithful believers.

After the pastor prayed, Dad tells us, "she got healed right away." She opened her eyes and accepted a bottle of milk, though a few minutes earlier, she had been barely breathing and nearly lifeless. God had healed her instantly!

In this feature, Dad tells us that was the first time he witnessed the Lord work in the life of his family by performing a miracle. As I heard him remembering the day on the cassette tape, I could hear his voice becoming emotional, and I imagined the warm pool of tears that had developed in the corners of his eyes. I felt my own tears well up upon hearing his voice quiver as he fought back tears.

With conviction in his voice, Dad explains that the Lord had planned to heal Ramona all along. Furthermore, he felt that God knew he needed to personally witness how the power of prayer could impact lives. Dad was not a Christian at the time, and God knew Dad needed to see a miracle in order to fortify his strength for the future, when he *would* become a believer. Letting Dad witness the baby's healing was part of God's master plan to soften and change his hardened heart.

Dad tells us that when they married, Mom was a follower of the teachings of Jesus Christ, and Dad had been raised in the Catholic church. He insists she did a lot of praying for him, and he knew that his mother—who loved him so much that she'd encouraged him to relocate his family from Texas to Ohio in hopes that Dad would realize he needed a drastic lifestyle adjustment—prayed for a change in him, too. Eventually, Dad saw the error of his ways and realized that Jesus was the only one who could save him and make him feel whole.

After the Lord began the work in Dad's heart, he learned to hear God's gentle voice and feel His gentle nudge, and he could sense the need to deliver personal messages to individuals when directed by the Holy Spirit. He believed that ministers could sense when they were supposed to give someone a message, because he experienced the same heightened awareness throughout his Christian walk. It was also evident to him that not all prayers were answered immediately. The prayer for his baby girl, thankfully, had been instantly gratifying.

Engrained in Dad's heart was the constant reminder that for him, living without Jesus in his heart was impossible. He spoke assuredly, knowing that he would be with Jesus when he finished his race on Earth. He had confidence in his voice and a peaceful demeanor when he talked about going home to be with Jesus—when the time was right, of course.

As a result of his being an active participant in the miracles the Lord allowed him to witness, providing inspirational testimonials became second nature to him. As the Lord's instrument, Dad could effectively deliver the message that God had the power to do anything. In addition, He promised we could do greater things than we could ever imagine by simply believing in the power when praying in the name of Jesus. Dad could sense God leading him into action with a gentle nudge on his conscience. With that same familiar nudge, Dad also knew how to pray or what to say to someone when there was a message to deliver.

Dad believed that when you learn about Jesus, trust in Him for your salvation, and do the best you can to live a Christian life, the Lord is alive within your soul. He spoke many times about how people only needed to obey the gentle voice of the Lord in order to be shown how to live a better life.

For a while, I struggled to make a decision as I worked on this project and this particular bit of my history. While running errands one day, I was pondering the choices available to me, when into my field of vision came the familiar signage on a truck with one word painted on its side: *Believe.* That one word renewed my faith that I was on the right path, and it made the choice clear for me. I had noticed the truck a few weeks earlier when contemplating a different decision related to this project. Both times I saw the truck, I felt the hair rise on my arms as goose bumps developed. The second time, I knew in my heart of hearts that I was experiencing a confirmation—a godsend, if you will—of the best kind.

As I retold the stories that Dad left for us to hear on cassette tape, it became increasingly evident that my life is mimicking Dad's. The Lord is using me as an instrument to chronicle Dad's experiences in order to bring the stories to light and honor the Lord. Dad clearly states that he is recording them for someone else to publish. God provided the experiences and people for him to encounter. Dad did the praying. God did the healing. Now I am doing the writing.

On that cold day in January 2015, after returning home from Dad's funeral, I was sitting in my La-Z-Boy recliner, bundled up in a quilt, when I experienced a visit from Dad, whom we had buried that morning. As I watched a TV show, I noticed movement out of the corner of my right eye, which I assumed was a piece of debris that I recognized as a floater. I cannot justify or explain what I saw, heard, and knew instantaneously during those few moments. I can tell you the visit was short, and it categorically did happen. Dad let me know that he was going to visit all seven of my siblings that day and that he was at peace. He was wearing his white baseball jacket and cap. With a *wink* of his left eye, he left my side as quickly as he had appeared. Like Santa beside a fireplace, he was gone. A sweet, calm, and peaceful feeling engulfed me. I wasn't sure what to make of the visit.

Within a few days, as I processed my experience, I felt comfortable enough to ask some of my siblings if they had gotten visits from Dad, too. No one had, but some wished they would have.

Is it a coincidence that as I edited his stories, I realized that the *wink* of Dad's eye carried meaning and produced a moment of clarity? He was assuring me that the cassette tape I'd received earlier that afternoon would be transcribed, written, and published as the book you are reading. Understanding the meaning behind his *wink* lifted my spirits and helped me step out in faith as an author, and I made the decision I had been struggling with the week before about how to publish this book. I was honored to be the instrument of God's choosing as I put the finishing touches on this collection of memories.

It just so happened that the above realization came to me on the fifth anniversary of Dad's passing.

On the cassette tape, this piece ends with Dad's signature closing: "Thank You, Jesus! Hallelujah!"

> *Again, I tell you this: If two of you agree on earth about anything*
> *you pray for, it will be done for you by My Father in heaven.*
> *For where two or three are gathered together in My name, there*
> *I am with them.* (**Matthew 18:19–20 NLV**)

CHAPTER 4

He Took Me Up to Heaven

On the tape recording, Dad continues sharing his knowledge and the experiences he had with Jesus Christ, including things Jesus showed him in a dream. In one dream, he saw heaven.

From the moment he established his spiritual relationship with Jesus Christ, he began to realize there was a plan for his life. A week and a half later, he got his second factory job at Tony's Sand Mold Company. Dad no longer had to work hard picking crops under the hot sun to support his family. He worked in that factory for fourteen years. Dad was proud to say, "I am a Christian!"

Dad liked to tell us that Jesus had his hand on him and protected him from all dangers. One of his favorite quotes from the Bible was "He will never leave us alone, or forsake us" (Hebrews 13:5). Jesus provided Dad with everything he needed at the right time.

One of the blessings God gave Dad early after he received Christ was a vision in the form of a dream. In that dream, the Lord took him to heaven in order to give him strength and more resolve to live for Him.

He was taken to the first floor of a room in heaven, where Jesus showed him beautiful things. Jesus said, *"This is the place where I want you to come be with me when it is time, because I am going to need you."*

Then he was taken to the second floor. Dad says, "There were beautiful things to see. I couldn't see very much because of the beauty and glory of the Lord. If you have a little time to think about heaven, you will figure out that it is a big place. I could see a room where the walls were thirty feet wide and forty feet long. I was able to see the size of the room very clearly. And I saw that it was a large place."

Dad continues recalling his vision by saying, "Then he took me to the third floor, or the third heaven, and there the beauty of the place was all that you could see. I couldn't see anything because of the beauty surrounding me. I saw beautiful lights of all kinds. The glory of the Lord was there! It was beautiful!"

Then the Lord spoke to him and asked if he could see the end of the room, where a light was glowing. Dad confirmed that he could see the glow and a big chair. The Lord explained that was where He was going to be when it was time to judge the people of Earth, and He wanted Dad to be there when it was time. He would bring Dad back to that place one day, he was told.

Dad felt he was given the vision of heaven so he would be motivated to continue trusting in Jesus and do his best to live a better life. Dad speaks of wanting to "get ready" and says he tried his best to live for Jesus and win souls for Him. Dad knew that if Jesus could change his heart, He could make a difference in other people's lives, too.

"He saved me so that I could work for Him," Dad says. "The Lord took me to that place to show me what heaven was like because He knew it would give me strength. I'm gonna tell you the truth!" he exclaims into the microphone. "In the name of Jesus! Hallelujah! Amen!"

> *I know a man who belongs to Christ. Fourteen years ago, he was taken up to the highest heaven. (I do not know if his body was taken up or just his spirit. Only God knows.) I say it again; I know this man was taken up. But I do not know if his body or just his spirit was taken up. Only God knows.*
> **(2 Corinthians 12:2–3 NLV)**

CHAPTER 5

You Gonna Fight with Jesus

After Dad's decision to surrender to the call of Christ in 1958, the Lord began to provide for him in ways that were new and different and that completely changed his life. He felt like a different man when God provided a factory job. While working in that new environment, he had to quickly learn how to live without substances; fighting, verbally or physically; and swearing, intentionally and unintentionally. His bad habits fell to the wayside as he tried his best to live a Christian life, especially the day a bully taunted him.

Within the factory workplace, he was forced to adapt to being around people of his faith and people of different faiths. Some of the nonbelievers laughed at him, made fun of him, and swore at him. Dad couldn't retaliate in kind, as he used to, because Jesus was in his heart, and his feelings and reactions toward others had changed.

One day one of his fellow workers made fun of him and swore at him a little more than usual. During the lunch break, that bully, who had been taunting him aggressively for several weeks, approached Dad from behind, grabbed his shoulders, and turned him so they were face-to-face. Then the bully grabbed one of Dad's shirt pockets and tore it off his shirt.

Dad is adamant when he tells us, "I know what I know! And I know what I believe! I had been telling this guy that if he wanted to pick a fight with me, you gonna fight with Jesus!"

Dad says that he felt himself go into a trance as he grabbed the bully by his shoulders. Then Dad lifted him up and slammed him onto the nearest cinder-block wall, banging him against it four times. He shook the man and forcefully said, "See? I told you! You not gonna fight with me; you gonna fight with Jesus!"

Then four of Dad's fellow workers came up to him and, with two on each arm, tried to make him release the bully. They begged Dad to leave him alone. But Dad was unable to let go of the bully, because the Lord was in control. Dad believed with all his heart that the Spirit of the Lord was in control of his body and was giving him the strength to lift the bully up onto the wall.

One of Dad's fellow workers asked, "What's the matter, Rivera?" Dad answered, "It's the Lord Jesus. It's not me!"

During the incident, Dad didn't hit the bully who had ripped off his shirt pocket. He just lifted him up onto the wall and held him there. He explained to the men who had come to help stop the would-be fight that he would loosen his hold on the bully when the Spirit of the Lord left his body.

When Dad was able to let the bully down, he reminded the bully of his previous words: "See? I told you. You not gonna fight with me; you gonna fight with Jesus!"

Over the years, Dad didn't share much about his workday when he was home, as he spent much of his time sleeping. He did bring home some of the working-man traits he learned from his fellow workers, including one that led us to teach *him* about a bad habit he had innocently learned at the factory.

This series of events must have happened when I was in high school; otherwise, I would not have been mature enough to understand the humor of the situation. One day Dad returned home after working a shift at the factory. I distinctly heard him say, "I gotta go take a sheet." I thought that was odd at the time because I didn't expect him to be helping Mom with the laundry that day, and that phrase was not something we were accustomed to saying in our home. The first day we heard him talk about the sheets like that, I heard giggles and snickering among my older siblings. Within the next few days, we heard him repeat the words about taking a sheet somewhere. Then came the jaw-dropping gasps, as he got up from where he had been seated and walked into the bathroom. We finally put two and two together: no pun intended.

Apparently, due to his poor English skills, the decline in his hearing capacity, and maybe even the element of a southern accent, Dad didn't realize that when fellow workers made that announcement in reference to their need to use the facility, the word he heard as *sheet* was actually a four-letter swear word. He simply heard them voice their need to use the bathroom. One of my brothers had to explain that Dad, by mimicking his fellow workers who needed to relieve themselves, had inadvertently been swearing all along. "Oh! I didn't know! I didn't know," he said, rather embarrassed. We all had fun laughing at him that afternoon, and he laughed at himself. Needless to say, that was the end of conversations about laundry and sheets in our household.

Dad ends this story with his signature, "Thank You, Jesus! Hallelujah!"

> *For if a man belongs to Christ, he is a new person. The old life is gone. New life has begun.* (**2 Corinthians 5:17 NLV**)

CHAPTER 6

Reyna Fall Down

D ad tells an account of a miracle that he and my siblings witnessed one spring day when he was returning us to school after we'd had lunch at home. In addition to being a stubborn eight-year- old, I exhibited other less-than-stellar character traits that day, and as a result, I am still learning life's lessons.

"Why do I have to help wash dishes? Mom never makes us wash dishes when we come home for lunch!" I sassed back to Dad after he ordered my seven siblings and me to clean up the kitchen before he drove us back to school after lunch on that cold, wet spring day.

Our previous daily routine of eating a packed lunch at school had changed recently because our stay-at-home mom was now a factory worker. The job enabled her to help make ends meet within the household. That day, Dad picked us up from school at noon so we could eat lunch at home. However, by making us clean up, Dad was cutting into my long thirty-minute recess time. The shorter morning and afternoon recesses lasted for fifteen minutes. Bitterness set into my tender heart, as my coveted long recess was not going to happen that day, and I was having nothing to do with it.

My siblings obeyed Dad and busied themselves with the task at hand. In my defiant anger, I pulled my green plaid wool coat over my thin cotton dress. Justifying my poor choices, I reasoned that if I started to walk the two miles to school immediately, I'd make it back before recess was over. After all, no one messed with my long recess period!

Off I went. I headed back to school on that chilly, wet spring day in my new white anklets, which Mom could now afford to buy at the five-and-ten-cent store, and black patent leather shoes from a secondhand store. As I tromped, I didn't know the mud puddles I was avoiding on County Road 90 would become important to me in just a few short minutes.

Up the hill I marched. I'd turn right at the Stop sign about a quarter of a mile away and make it to school on time. I was sure that no one had noticed my absence.

As I trudged up the country road, I complained to myself about having a lazy father. In my eyes, I thought he was trying to get out of doing dishes so he could lie down for a nap sooner after he drove us back to school. In my recollection of this blow-by-blow explanation nearly sixty years later, I'm certain he needed all the extra nap time he could get as he juggled work and a brood of seven kids. The old adage of learning something new every day applies here in more ways than one. I have learned the value of a power nap. I have also learned the value of initiating difficult conversations with people I love before it is too late.

Seemingly, the Stop sign literally instructed me to stop all my foolishness at the top of the hill. I had sassed Dad and defied him, and now I was bitter and determined. That resulted in guilt. The guilt made me turn my head to look back to my home. A new reality set in. I saw my siblings outside the house, piling into the car. I wasn't going to beat everyone back to school unless I abandoned my mission and ran back home. Because of my cold and bitter heart, I had cold feet—literally—inside those secondhand shoes that day. My legs and feet warmed up quickly as I shamefully ran back down the hill, unaware that my actions would result in dire consequences I would remember for a lifetime.

I had been a disrespectful, disobedient girl who defiantly decided to attempt to walk to school. Heading home, I felt remorseful and winded, but glad that I'd be riding in the car to head back to school and still have time for recess. Upon my return I entered the already open door to get into the back seat of the four-door 1952 Chevy and pulled the heavy, cumbersome door behind me. I was not aware that in my haste, I had failed to close the back door of the car securely. I had instead focused my attention on the fact that a younger sister had noticed my retreat from the road and tattled of my return to Dad. He didn't respond to her and that was good for me.

Growing up in a large household necessitated an established pecking order for self-survival, even when riding in a car. Speaking of survival, there were no seat belts in cars back then. That day, our two oldest brothers sat in the front passenger seating area. Arrangements for sitting in the rear passenger area involved an every-girl-for-herself routine. If we remembered and were quick enough, we would call for a window seat. When the seating area was filled, there was standing room only. That day, I was standing by the rear right-side door.

By that time, everyone was urging Dad to hurry and get us back to school for the precious few minutes left of our long lunch recess. He moved the gear shift into reverse then quickly stepped on the gas pedal to back out of the muddy driveway. Immediately, he turned the steering wheel to turn left onto the road. Centrifugal force generated by the speed of the turning car moving in reverse pushed all the children riding in the back of the car—seated and standing—toward me, propelling my body against the door and ejecting me onto the road.

Remember the puddles? I landed in a soft, cold, muddy tire-track depression. The next few seconds happened quickly. I can still feel the weight of the car compressing my chest. I can hear the thump of the tire as it passed from the left side of my lower chest cavity, angling across the middle of my chest, before it ended its track over my right shoulder. My head was turned to the left, so the tire missed my head. Had I been in the wrong place at the wrong time? Or the right place at the right time? God's timing is, indeed, everything!

Dad's love of Jesus is the saving grace in this story. In recording the saga on the cassette tape, he tells his listeners, "One of my daughters—she opened the car door." He exclaims, "Reyna fall down! She fell on the road!"

Dad had faith in the power of prayer. When he saw me lying in the mud puddle with a crushed chest, he knew it was too late. I was dead. His faith in a living God prompted him to lay his hands on me in prayer. His obedient children followed his commands to kneel in the mud, bow their heads, and close their eyes as he prayed, "Lord, you know she belongs to this family. But if it is your will, heal her completely. If not, I will give her to you on this highway. But somehow, someway, I want you to answer our prayers."

"But, if it is your will," I heard him say on the tape recording. The moment I heard those words spoken on the cassette tape, I realized that my dad had been willing to relinquish his earthly ties with me as I laid on the road. Yet his faith had guided him to ask Jesus to bring me back to life. That prayer of faith resulted in this retelling. The themes of "somehow, someway" and "Jesus can use you" resonate clearly in Dad's recordings.

In Dad's version, he says he thought it was too late. I was dead.

I didn't hear angels sing. I heard my oldest brother yell, "Dad! You ran over Reyna!"

I don't remember Dad directing my siblings to kneel for prayer in the mud puddle. I don't remember Dad putting his hands around me as he declared to Jesus that I belonged to this family here on Earth but that if it was God's will, he would give me to Him right there on the highway. Neither did I hear him say that he wanted Jesus to answer his prayer. It wasn't until I began transcribing Dad's recordings that I thought of the drama that had occurred as a miracle.

After the prayer of faith, Dad and my oldest brother picked me up from the mud and put me on the front passenger seat of the car, and Dad drove the mile or so to the local clinic. I can't imagine the guilt, fear, and sadness that must have hung heavily in the car.

My memory of the view of the front of the clinic building through the front windshield is vivid. I recall hearing that we were to drive to the back door, where the doctor would meet us. The next thing I knew, I was looking at a large, bright light overhead, and Dr. Louis was telling Dad there was nothing wrong with me. Dad walked over to the chair in the corner of the room, picked up the little plaid green coat I had been wearing, and showed him the muddy tire track to prove that there had indeed been an accident and that he had run over my chest with the car. Dad thought that if he showed the doctor my coat, his account of the incident would be more believable.

My school-age siblings were able to go back to school that afternoon. I got to rest on the sofa at home. When Mom got home from work, someone informed her about the events of the day, and life went back to normal. Dad never knew the totality of how I had defied him that day. I had heard my sister tattle that I had been on the road. He never acknowledged my insolence. In his version of his memory, while he was backing left out of the driveway to get on the highway, I opened the back door on purpose. In reality, I had never even opened the door to get into the car.

I had been too busy running home with those new little white-laced anklets tucked inside my little Mary Janes. Someone else had opened the rear right-side door of the car, and I happened to be the last one to climb into the rear passenger area.

Before I learned Dad's version of what he knew to be the truth, I would boast that from that day forward, we were allowed to eat lunch at school. As I sat at the lunch table the first day that I was allowed to return to school, a fellow student spoke to me in passing and asked if I was the little girl who had been run over by a car. Smiling at him, I boastfully answered, "Yes," knowing I was going to be able to have my long recess after lunch and I had survived falling out of a moving car—in reverse, no less!

But now, as a result of learning life's lessons, I have learned not to gloat when I retell this part of my life now that Dad's rendition of the afternoon has filled in the blanks. Now I'm humbled to know I was a participant in a miracle.

As I listened to Dad talk about the event and reviewed the typed script, I was reminded that he wanted this incident exposed as evidence of his faith in a living God. Dad believed that Jesus was the Son of God and was sent to Earth so we could have the chance to believe in the simplicity of it all. Dad asks us to acknowledge a higher power who somehow sent an only Son to Earth in the form of a man. Perhaps for some readers, the path to believing Dad's message is not cut and dry. Science and common sense might prevail over literal translations concerning creationism and events in the Bible. Nonetheless, I am a living witness of and participant in this undeniable testimony of how we were both used to glorify the living God.

Hindsight tells me that Dad carried the guilt of running over me with the car for the rest of his life. He feared he had caused his daughter's death.

In reality, I had set the scene for the accident to happen. I had disrespected Dad when I sassed him. I'd disobeyed Dad by not helping with the dishes. I had coveted my recess time. My attempt to walk back to school had failed. After running back home, I had failed to close the car door properly as I climbed into the car. I had developed bitterness, defiance, stubbornness, and selfishness at the age of eight. As I sit at this keyboard, putting Dad's words into manuscript form so his dream of putting his stories into print will become a reality, I am still learning lessons from that fateful day.

My would-be tragedy was the second life-and-death miracle he participated in and witnessed during his lifetime. In each life-and-death scenario my dad experienced, prayer and faith resulted in family members being brought back to life.

In Dad's stories, he repeats one simple theme, followed by a request. There is a Spiritual Being. His name is Jesus, and He is the Son of God. One day life brought my father to a point where he admitted helplessness. Not knowing what else to do, Dad talked to the Spiritual Being about the troubled feelings in his soul.

We all know that place within ourselves, even though modern technology is still unable to detect it as a body part. We all feel it within. We cannot touch, see, or hold it. Even so, we are able to open or close the door to our soul at will.

If your life's journey brings you to a place where you are helpless and don't know what to do, Dad suggested that you begin your one-sided conversation with that Spiritual Being, whatever name you give It. Keep your talk simple. State facts clearly. Ask for a change of heart. I can't explain the change that will happen, but I can tell you that the feeling is real, and the change happens in that intangible body part we call the soul.

The lessons I began learning that day as an eight-year-old have now come full circle as a result of my calling forth my memories and putting them in printed form. My immature thinking skills as an eight-year-old led me to make decisions that have impacted my life to this day. Today I know that lack of obedience can lead to consequences as I struggle with the feelings of guilt of never having had a discussion about my disobedience and the resulting accident with Dad. I cannot imagine the daily torment he must have felt after he ran over my body with the car. What heartache and despair he must have felt! It is my hope that those feelings abated over time.

As I grew, when I happened to get an ache or pain, Dad would ask me how I felt. He never mentioned the accident, but I had a feeling that the accident was the reason he was asking.

It is too late for me to provide the shameful, embarrassing missing details that would have filled in the sequence of events and allowed him to fully understand the events of that day. However, I often feel his spirit next to me, and I have faith that he knows the truth. I can imagine his response.

If I could go back in time, I'd begin a conversation with him by saying, "Dad, tell me about the time you ran over me with the car. There are a few details you need to know. I want you to know everything about that day. But first, I want to hear your voice one more time as you tell the story in your own words."

I can see myself sitting in a chair beside Dad as he bows his head, and the silver threads of his thinning hair sparkle when he nods. He is working hard to dredge up the painful memories of that day. The aging, loose skin on his neck moves as he swallows the thickness building in his throat, indicating he knows that what I have asked him to recount will not be produced without guilt releasing tears. I can hear him take a breath as he lifts his weary head, and then he looks into the window of my soul with his tired and faded soft brown eyes. He takes a few cleansing breaths, digs deep into his thoughts, and becomes curious about why I have asked. He senses that I need to hear it for a special reason. Then he feels the familiar gentle nudge of the Spirit of the Lord, which is ready to guide him as he fulfills my request. I don't interrupt his narrative. When he is finished telling me his accounting, I fill in the missing additional details. Afterward, I humbly remember to confess, "I'm sorry I was disobedient that day. Thank you for praying that prayer of faith and asking Jesus to let me live."

Then, I pretend, he lowers his head and squints just a bit, as if in deep thought. Slowly his lips tighten and then begin to quiver, and he does not fight back the emotion welling up in his throat. Softly, emotional words tumble off his tongue as cleansing tears run down his cheeks. He says, "Thank you. Thank you. Don't worry about it mi'jita. It happened a long time ago, and you were just a little girl. Anyway, I thank Jesus for the woman you have become. I love you."

Honor your father and your mother, so your life may be long in the land the Lord your God gives you. (**Exodus 20:12 NLV**)

CHAPTER 7

Her Name Is Renata

The explanation that follows provides a snapshot of the circumstances that arose after the birth of our youngest brother, Rolando, who was born on Monday, June 10, 1963. At the age of thirty-eight my mom, Renata, had a life-and-death experience due to complications associated with the delivery of her last child. Dad's thirty-seventh birthday was the next day, Tuesday, June 11, 1963.

Dad claimed his spiritual birth date as Saturday, June 14, 1958. Five months later, Mom delivered her eighth child on November 26, 1958, and they named the baby boy Rodrigo. Unfortunately, he died shortly after birth. Five years after Dad gave his life to Christ, Mom delivered her ninth—and last—child, a baby boy. After the delivery, Mom's bleeding could not be controlled; hemorrhaging led to a complete hysterectomy. On Tuesday morning, the doctors called Dad to give him the news that they'd had to perform emergency surgery in order to attempt to save Mom's life. Sadly, after surgery, her medical condition worsened, and the situation became even more critical.

The duration of the family crisis was undeterminable, so we were shifted from one family's home to another until we could return home. There were seven children living at home, and we were divided by twos or threes and sent to stay with our uncle in the neighboring town or were temporarily sent to the homes of church members to be cared for a few days at a time.

Dr. Laurie was the attending physician. He donated thirteen pints of blood over the course of four days in order to help make a positive difference in Mom's deteriorating health. On Tuesday morning, after informing Dad of Mom's worsening critical medical condition, the doctor informed Dad that he needed to begin the process of deciding which funeral home he would use, as death was imminent. Dad was to tell the hospital which funeral home to take her body to, because the prognosis was death.

Rolando had been born on Monday, and now it was Saturday. The doctor disclosed to Dad that there had been no change in Mom's condition. On Sunday morning, the doctor approached Dad again, wanting an answer. "Mr. Rivera, which funeral home did you make arrangements with? We need to know where to send your wife's body after she passes away."

Dad answered the doctor by saying, "Doctor, I haven't made up my mind about a funeral home yet."

It had now been a week since Mom had given birth. On Monday morning at nine o'clock, Dr. Laurie approached Dad again. This time, the message was more difficult for the doctor to deliver. "I'm sorry to tell you, Mr. Rivera, your wife just passed away. Please accept my sincere condolences."

Dad ignored the announcement of her death and answered, "Doctor, I want you to give me permission to go see my wife."

He replied, "I'm sorry, Mr. Rivera. It's too late. She is dead. There is no reason for you to go see her. Have you decided which funeral home you will be using?"

Ignoring the question about the funeral home selection, Dad exclaimed, "I don't care if she's dead. Just let me go see her!"

Our family pastor had been keeping vigil with Dad at the hospital, and when the doctor informed Dad that Mom had passed away, the pastor spoke up and insisted the doctor grant them permission to see Mom's body. The doctor tried to discourage them from seeing Mom's body, again by telling them both, "It's too late!"

But the minister was persistent and replied, "No, it's not too late!"

Out of the kindness of his heart, the doctor relented and led them to the second floor of the hospital. He asked them to wait for a few minutes while he went into one of the rooms. Then he returned, informing them that they had permission to see her body; however, they had to limit their time to five minutes, as staff members were waiting to prepare her body before transporting her to the funeral home of Dad's choice.

Dad's explanation of why Mom died is simple: "She could not hold blood in her body." He also reminds his listeners that the Bible says, "Blood is life."

Continuing his explanation, Dad indicates that he understood exactly what the Lord wanted him to do and say at that moment. He explained to the doctor that he understood that his wife was dead, but he and the pastor wanted to go lay their hands on her in prayer.

There on the second floor of Memorial Hospital on Loop Street, widower Rianco and the minister entered the room where Mom's lifeless body lay on the gurney. In the room with Mom's body were two nurses, one on each side of her body, and two male attendants, one at her head and one at her feet, ready to follow protocol. The hospital employees were there to prepare the corpse, an everyday occurrence in their chosen profession. The body they were attending had emptied itself of its life-giving blood. The staff members could not have imagined what they would witness in the next few minutes.

Dad tells us that he and the minister began their prayers by laying their hands on the top of Mom's head. The Holy Spirit and the healing power of the Lord entered the room as they prayed reverently, expectantly, and, most of all, obediently. The Lord had shown Dad how to pray, and He guided his every word. The Bible tells us that no words spoken by God are ever wasted.

Dad didn't leave us an account of what the attending hospital staff did while he and the minister said their prayers. I wonder if they bowed their heads in respect and kept their eyes on Mom's body. Maybe they said their own prayers. Perhaps they felt sorry for the new widower because they understood the inevitable: she was no longer alive.

I know with a moral certainty that the reverend and Dad closed their eyes and bowed their heads as Dad poured out his heart to God, saying, "Lord, I know that I need my wife. Lord, I got seven kids at home, and here in the hospital there is another one. That's gonna be eight kids to care for. What can I do with eight kids? I need my wife. I ask you to give her back to me. I want you to bring her back! In the name of Jesus, I pray. Amen!"

I cannot tell you what happened next and give justice to the miracle, so I have decided to include Dad's full text, which follows:

The Holy Spirit, the healing power of the Lord, came down from heaven. We touched her head at the same time, me and the preacher. And the Lord really came through for us that time! The Lord brought her back after the doctor told us that she was dead!

And then I tell you that somehow, somewhere, I don't know where the blood came from, because her body was dry. It didn't have any blood in it. That's why she had died—because she didn't have blood in her body. But Jesus is the one that put the blood back into her body. He put blood into her body to bring her back from the dead. And somehow, somewhere, the Lord put the blood back into her body.

Dad continues his recollection by telling us that the Lord blessed them when they had finished praying. The minister and Dad were hollering and crying. With a grateful heart Dad uttered the words, "Thank You, Jesus, for healing my wife. Thank You for bringing her back!"

While they were hollering and crying, Mom opened her eyes. The nurses shook their heads as they stood on either side of Mom's now-living body. She was a corpse no longer. Blood was flowing through her body.

As the daughter and storyteller today, I would love to hear the accounts from the nurses and staff who witnessed the miracle that the minister and my dad—a simple man who was a believer—were part of that day. If the staff members could add their words to this memoir, what would they say? Would they talk about how their own lives changed the day they witnessed the miracle of death and life at Memorial Hospital on Loop Street?

This is one of several major miracles Dad witnessed while he was living for the Lord and doing his best to live the life of an obedient Christian. Dad liked to say, "The Lord has power to do anything!"

As powerful as the miracle was, I don't recall hearing Mom or Dad offer this account of how the Lord answered his simple prayer. In relaying the description on the cassette tape, he says simply, "And that's how my wife came back from the dead. The Lord brought her back that way."

After that experience, Dad knew that the Lord could use him and that He would do things when asked. Dad believed and knew firsthand that he could ask the Lord to do greater things than he himself, as a believer, could ever imagine. He was adamant that if we ask for things in Jesus's name, then indisputable, unbelievable things can be done simply because Jesus promised his believers that all they had to do was believe when they asked for things in His name.

Dad was overwhelmed with joy when he opened his eyes after praying and heard one of the nurses announce, "Mr. Rivera, your wife is living! She's going to live!"

When they were instructed to leave her side and go to the waiting room of the hospital so she could be attended to, they were both still overjoyed, and their tears flowed freely because the Lord continued to bless them. They cried because they had seen a miracle performed by Jesus. Jesus had given Mom life again!

While they were in the waiting room, Dr. Laurie energetically approached Dad and said, "Mr. Rivera, I want to shake your hand!"

Dad was humbled that the doctor had gone out of his way to find him in order to shake his hand. Dad remembers saying, "Doctor, what did you say?"

"I want to shake your hand!" he repeated.

Dad replied, "Doctor, I'm always gonna remember what you did for my wife! Her name was Renata."

The jubilant doctor continued his conversation with Dad, informing him, "They are going to remove all the tubes and needles from your wife's body so she can start living again. We will keep her in the hospital another week or so until she gets stronger. Then we will send her home to be with your family and the new baby."

Weeks later, the doctor informed Dad that he had tried to save Mom's life for four hours by taking it upon himself to be the donor during a necessary blood transfusion. He confessed that over the course of her stay, he had donated a total of thirteen pints of blood as Mom fought for her life. His actions proved to Dad that he was a great man and a perfect doctor for Mom.

That experience made Dad's faith even stronger. He knew and believed that his Lord was able to answer prayer. He knew firsthand that Jesus would never fail him or leave him alone with life's daily struggles. In Dad's own words, he tells us, "I want to give glory to Him. Because He is the one that did the healing. I'm not. I prayed for the people, but Jesus used me. I prayed in the name of Jesus so that the Lord could heal people. The Lord is the one that healed the people I prayed for."

By retelling the account of this miracle, I am reminded that Dad's testimonies in audio-recorded form never fail to remind us that his experiences with Jesus Christ were many. God changed lives by guiding Dad to become a prayer warrior. Dad loved an audience willing to listen to his testimonies of God's love. If he was testifying in church, the preacher would have to remind him that time for sharing was over. Dad would be the first one to tell you he could talk all day and all night and still have stories to share about what the Lord had done for him and others.

Dad tells us that two weeks after delivering her last child, Mom was able to come home. He was thankful that she was living. And she was thrilled to be alive!

Dad's account on the cassette tape continues:

> My wife lived for forty years after receiving that healing in her body. I thank the Lord because He gave her back to me when I needed her more than ever. Because in the days when she was sick, I had a lot of kids. The Lord brought her back. The Lord gave her back to me because I needed my wife. And I thank the Lord for that.
>
> If it were not for my wife, I would probably not be alive, because I was a drunker. I was an *alcoholico*! But it was the Lord's plan to save my soul!

Dad didn't have to decide which funeral home to send her to until she passed away nearly forty years later.

Dad ends this saga with his signature praise: "Thank You, Jesus! Hallelujah!"

> *If you get your life from Me and My Words live in you, ask whatever you want. It will be done for you.* (**John 15:7 NLV**)

CHAPTER 8

Just Enough Time

At this point in his recording sessions, Dad doesn't seem to tire of continuing to share his Christian testimony, and he wants to share "one more little testimony" about a road trip via car that he made with Mom. Although they were traveling alone from Ohio to Texas during their golden years as empty-nesters, they were reminded that they were never really alone. They lived together as a married couple for more than fifty years before God took Mom to heaven. Wherever they traveled, God would go before them. As Dad would say, "He would keep his hands on us."

In Dad's younger days, he recalls, he was able to drive from the little town in Ohio to Texas within a twenty-five-hour time frame. As time progresses, he speaks about "driving all day and night."

When that particular trip took place, they decided to begin their trip from Ohio on a Sunday night, after church services were over. He tells us they waited until the last chorus of the last song was near its end before walking out of the sanctuary. Earlier during the service, prayer requests had been solicited, and they had announced that their trip would begin at the close of service, which had prompted the preacher to include a request for their safe travel during his intercessory prayer time.

Dad tells us that he drove all night, through the next day, and into the night again, when the incident happened. Research helped me narrow the date of the trip to between 1960 and 1970, as a portion of the northbound and southbound road construction for Route 55 in Illinois was finished by May 1966. I deduced that at least part of Route 55 from Saint Louis,

Missouri, to Kato, Illinois, was incomplete, as Dad talks about trying to pass a semitruck while traveling on a two-lane road. At that point in time, Route 55 from Saint Louis to Kato would have indeed been the dangerous, hilly two-lane road Dad talks about. He voiced his concern to Mom, and he indicates that he knew extreme care while driving was imperative because of the high probability of danger.

It was two o'clock in the morning, and Dad had been following a semitruck, which seemed to go even slower as the driver changed gears to navigate the elevated, climbing grades. The long drive had begun to wear on his patience, and he wanted nothing more than to pass the semitruck. He asked Mom, "Honey, do you think I can pass this semi?"

After he asked her three times, she said, "Well, you can try it, but be careful."

At that point in the adventure, the prayers offered by the pastor prior to their travel were about to bring forth fruit. Dad had made up his mind. He decided to pass the semitruck while they were climbing a hill. He moved into the left lane to pass, and surprisingly, a second semitruck appeared in his view. It had been in front of the first truck he had been following, and he hadn't been aware of its position. Then my parents saw the stomach-wrenching danger at the same moment in time: a third semitruck was coming at them from the opposite direction!

Dad is animated as he describes the situation: "And, man, I tell you that the Lord came through with us that night! My car was running at fifty-five to sixty miles an hour, when I saw the bright lights of the semi coming towards us. I don't know what happened! But it looked like the Lord took control of my car and moved it to the left side of the road. There was a big cut in the stone on the side of the mountain. The Lord put my car at the only place where there was just enough space for the semi to pass through without hitting our car!"

His voice takes on an incredulous tone as he continues with the following account: "After the truck passed our car, my wife and I could not speak! I asked her, 'Are you okay, Honey?' She answered, 'Yes, I'm all right.'"

They couldn't understand what had happened. When they came to a stop, they saw that their car lights were still on. They also knew that the car motor was running, because he had been attempting to pass both semitrucks. The only answer possible was divine intervention. The Lord had answered the prayer the pastor had offered during the church service before they'd left their hometown. It was evident the Lord had been with them throughout that dangerous near-miss. Their car had had just enough time to pass on the left side of the road, the oncoming semitruck didn't hit the side of the mountain and all four vehicles continued traveling without impact!

My parents were both in shock—so much so that they could not speak. When they were able to talk again a few minutes later, Dad said, "Look at what just happened! Do you know what happened?"

"No, I don't know. I know the semi was gonna hit us!" Mom replied in amazement.

Dad was convinced that the Lord had guided all the vehicles that night. He also felt strongly that without the Lord's hand, an accident would have occurred and resulted in their fatalities. Each of them "would have been with Jesus already," instead of telling us this story.

They took a few minutes to rest and say a prayer of thanks before preparing to drive again. The car key was in the off position, and the motor was not running. After he felt calm enough to begin driving again, Dad started the motor and then watched carefully as he slowly backed up, because they were so close to the mountain.

It was evident the Lord had intervened with the traffic on Route 55 that night. He remembers telling Mom, "Look! The key is pointing up, and my lights are on! Thank the Lord because He saved our lives tonight!"

That night, they were happy to be alive, and they couldn't sleep. As they drove through the darkness, they could feel the calming, reassuring presence of the Lord. Dad gave thanks to Jesus for that testimony. To him, it seemed, "the Lord took [his] car off the highway with a magnet and put it on the side of the road." He says, "I'm glad for that because the Lord came through for us and kept us safe! I know that we were trying the best we could to live for Him. The Lord returned goodness through our preacher's prayer for safe travel."

After unfolding that drama, Dad reminds us, "The Lord is always with us! He never leaves us alone! He never forsakes us!"

I could tell that story brought up vivid memories for Dad. I heard his unsteady, shaky voice. I could almost see his lip quiver and the rise and fall of his Adam's apple before it rested in its neutral position as he delivered his account with grateful emotion.

"Tonight, I just gonna stop here because I know that the Lord is here with me. And probably tomorrow I finish this tape. Okay? And I see you tomorrow," he says. Then he adds in classic Dad style with a twist, "Thank You, Jesus. And good night, Jesus! Hallelujah!"

> *Because you have made the Lord your safe place, and the Most High the place where you live, nothing will hurt you. No trouble will come near your tent. For He will tell His angels to care for you and keep you in all your ways. They will hold you up in their hands. So, your foot will not hit against a stone.* **(Psalm 91:9–12 NLV)**

CHAPTER 9

Bring Him Back

The Lord can work wonders and use His believers wherever they go. As Dad was driving his car one day, he encountered a traffic accident, and God gently drew him closer to the scene and directed him to use a prayer of faith to help a victim. I feel that I am traveling alongside Dad, as I, too, am drawn to follow a predestined path and retell his life's interactions with people. We both have traveled on the right path.

It was that quiet time filled with anxiety after a traffic accident happened on the highway within viewing range. People stopped their cars along the side of the road. A traveler arrived just after the sound of metal crashing against metal. That person got out of his car, began to access the surreal events of the day, and called the local rescue or police department to report the accident.

At the end of that warm summer day, dusk was beginning to settle in southern Ohio. Tomas, a local businessman, was one of the first to arrive at the scene, and he happened to be a volunteer on the rescue squad. He made the necessary calls to contact the police department so that assistance could begin on State Route 40 West, just past the popular Twisty-Cone.

My dad was one of the curious travelers who, along with a growing number of others, exited his vehicle and cautiously decided to get a closer look at the activity unfolding before him. Bravely, they stepped closer, anxiously hoping that with each step they would discover that no one in their families had been involved in the accident before them.

At first glance, they didn't notice the small tree along the road that had been cut in half and lay splintered and broken in pieces in the patch of weeds. No one noticed the distinct impression of a car's hubcap burnished into a telephone pole where the car's tire had hit just a few minutes earlier or the bits of glass scattered on the road, lying shattered among the gravel, dirt, and warm, glistening blood on the toe of a small shoe.

Instead, people took note of the color and make of the vehicles involved, breathing sighs of relief when they didn't recognize the vehicles in the aftermath of the crash. Deep inside each person was a feeling of sadness for the victims but also personal comfort and relief in the realization that a precious family member had not been involved in the accident.

As Dad approached the scene, which he seemed drawn to, he saw a large amount of blood beside one particular victim, a young boy with dark hair and dark skin. The fresh bruises on his forehead were beginning to swell. Blood along a large, gaping cut at his scalp had pressed his hair into a slick, wet mat. Dad smelled the scent of the young boy's blood in the air.

Being careful not to step on anything sharp or jagged or the shoe that had landed several yards away from the scene, Dad made his way through the people gathered to stand near Tomas, the rescue-squad volunteer. Tomas seemed to have taken it upon himself to keep onlookers from disturbing anything or anyone involved. Dad knew him by name because he was his insurance agent. Dad decided—no, knew—that the little boy lying in a pool of his own warm blood needed prayer, so he approached the volunteer rescue-team member.

As Tomas and Dad stood there looking at the terrible scene, Dad shared his thought aloud: "I want to pray for that little boy."

"Why?" replied the stunned man.

"The Lord is gonna heal him," Dad answered with conviction. The man asked incredulously, "How do you know?"

In his broken English, Dad said, "Because I just *know* the Lord is gonna heal him."

Dad was a man of faith and had had firsthand experiences as a participant in and witness to several life-and-death miracles during his Christian walk with Jesus Christ. He didn't have qualms about humbling himself in prayer during any given public situation. That day, on the main road leading in and out of that little village, things were no different. He felt the need to pray immediately and was willing to kneel in prayer in front of the onlookers, who were strangers to each other and to him, at the scene of the surreal accident. Dad felt that offering a prayer was the only thing he could give in the way of assistance. He wanted and felt compelled to pray for the child, whose eyes were swollen shut and who was missing his right shoe, and he was not ashamed to offer a prayer to request divine intervention in front of the strangers.

There along the highway, among his insurance agent and all the other curious onlookers, Dad humbled himself and began to talk to Jesus. Kneeling down in the midst of brokenness, Dad placed his hand gently under the little boy's head, closing his own eyes and opening his heart and mouth to begin a prayer in the only language he knew that others would understand: his broken English. "Lord, I am here with these people looking down at this little boy, and we can see that he's hurt. You know that he is in bad condition, but I pray that somehow you can touch him from the top of his head to the soles of his feet. And, Lord, I pray that somehow you can make him whole. Bring him back. In the name of Jesus, I pray. Amen." That was his simple prayer.

The people gathered witnessed the humble act of a simple man who boldly uttered a simple prayer of faith from the depths of his grateful heart. After the prayer, the little boy did not miraculously stop bleeding, get up from the highway, and walk away. This miracle didn't happen like a scene in a made-for-TV movie. Dad had been known to remind us that sometimes, when a believer says a prayer, he or she might have to wait for it to be answered by God in a timely manner.

Perhaps the onlookers wished they had bowed their heads and closed their own eyes in respect while my dad knelt in prayer. Maybe they kept their eyes open and were witness to a man who knelt in prayer in the midst of a traffic scene, making the horrible sight even more surreal. Yet somehow, they probably felt a calmness that was hard to explain.

When Dad finished his prayer and thanked Jesus for healing the little boy, he felt the Lord's blessing. Because the power of the Lord was so great within him, warm tears ran down his cheeks, marking the emotional blessing and afterglow of the Spirit of the Lord. Then, as gently as the Spirit of the Lord had entered Dad's body during that act of obedient prayer, it gently and sweetly left him.

Dad turned to Tomas and reassuringly said, "The boy is gonna be all right. I asked the Lord to heal him completely."

A few days later, Dad and Mom contacted Tomas to ask where the emergency squad had taken the little boy. They learned he had been taken to Community Hospital in the neighboring town and decided to visit him there.

When Dad entered the little boy's hospital room and began a conversation, the boy recognized Dad's voice. With a big smile on his face, he said, "You are the man that prayed for me that day when I was laying on the highway!"

"Yes, I am the one," Dad said.

"I could hear every word you said during your prayer. I know that I was in bad shape. But look here—I'm all right! They found out that I don't have any broken bones. There is nothing wrong with my body!" the boy proudly exclaimed.

In recording this account on the cassette tape, Dad says, "The Lord had performed a miracle for that little boy. The doctors didn't find any broken bones or anything like that. That is because when we pray and we belong to Jesus, He promised that we can ask for *greater* things, and they will be given unto us. He lives in our hearts, you know."

Dad continues telling about the hospital visit. He spoke to the little boy about salvation and God's love for mankind. The little boy replied, "Well, I don't know too much about Jesus. I want to tell you about something. I used to live in Detroit, Michigan."

Tears welled up in the corners of his dark brown eyes as he showed Dad and Mom the scars on his arms. He had endured physical and verbal abuse while in that city. His arms were scarred with burns where others had pressed the hot stubs of marijuana cigarettes—which he'd refused to smoke—into his young, tender flesh. When the boy had refused their demands, they had reacted by punishing him with cigarette burns.

After the boy unburdened himself of his painful memories, Dad had words of encouragement for him in the form of a closing prayer. This time, Dad was able to pray with the young boy while the little boy respectfully closed his dark brown eyes by his own choosing.

During the visit, Dad advised the little boy not to lose heart and added, "The Lord is gonna use you. You got a testimony for this."

Dad closes this session by saying, "I know the Lord can do a lot of things like that. In the name of Jesus. Hallelujah!"

As I chronicle Dad's stories, I am in awe of how his original cassette tape, which he recorded while sitting under the shade tree at the old homestead where he and Mom raised eight children, traveled from his hand to mine after his funeral five years ago. I think of this project as a divinely choreographed sequence of events that have been recorded and preserved. It seems odd to me that for some unknown reason, I don't think of this project as work or a dreaded task to be finished. It doesn't hang over my head and control my every thought, nor does it keep me awake at night. I will confess that when I do awaken at night, I often have fresh thoughts that I weave into the script. Dad knew that the Lord was going to heal the little boy before he prayed for him. In the same way, I know that transferring Dad's stories from oral to printed form is something that has always been my predestination.

I have heard people say that they love the work they do for a living and are lucky to have jobs they love, because if you love your job, it doesn't feel like work. Now I can say that I truly know the meaning of their words. A friend reminded me that a greater power predetermined that I would perform this work. Every skill I have needed to perform my calling has been practiced and perfected. Everything I have needed has been provided: I obtained the cassette tape and transferred the audio from cassette to CD format with the help of a friend; I learned to break down the audio into sound bites; family and friends agreed to read parts of the script and provide feedback or volunteered to edit; and finally, I found a writing buddy.

My writing skills have grown one step at a time, beginning with Mom teaching me to write my name. Then my kindergarten teacher, Mrs. Albesa showed me how to write the English spelling (Rayna) of my Spanish name (Reyna). Subsequent to that, my second-grade teacher, Mrs. Santos asked my class to draw a picture of our fathers working at their jobs. I drew my father working at Tony's Sand Mold Company. Mom would drive my siblings and me to the factory when she took Dad his supper. There I watched him pull levers and turn switches to make sand molds. I drew my picture of him doing just that. He was wearing a green uniform with a Tony's Sand Mold Company patch on his left breast pocket. I drew him standing at his work station, pulling levers and pushing buttons. I labeled my picture "Daddy making money," because when I'd asked my dad what he did at his job, he'd said, "I make money."

After I married and moved six hours from the homestead, I began to handwrite family addresses into an address book so I wouldn't lose track of my siblings and their children. Later, I entered the addresses and other family data onto spreadsheet cells. These days, while I work on my genealogy, I enter data into a private software program. At every turn, when I have put words onto paper, I have gained new writing skills. Those steps strengthened and enhanced the writing skills I needed to share Dad's Christian testimony with others.

One day I answered a telephone call from my friend Gwen, who had been editing my manuscript, and she let me know that it was ready for pickup. After tirelessly editing my first attempt at writing a piece for the fourth time, she commented that she finally felt the freedom to make constructive edits. When I picked up the edited manuscript, I asked her if she had been able to effectively edit my manuscript or if she was holding back so as not to hurt my feelings. Her response was insightful as she said, "There was no need to edit as much because I could tell you are more comfortable with your writing. You have found your voice and are on the right path."

> *The prayer given in faith will heal the sick man, and the Lord will raise him up. If he has sinned, he will be forgiven.* (**James 5:15 NLV**)

CHAPTER 10

Right Time Right Place

Just like the TV character Miles Finer, played by Brandon Micheal Hall, on the new American comedy drama series *God Friended Me*, which began airing on Sunday nights, my dad found himself becoming an agent of change as God intervened in his life to answer prayers and change the lives of people he encountered.

"Where do you think she is in this hospital?" Dad asked Mom as they walked into the medical center in a small Texas community in 1996.

My parents spent the winter seasons visiting relatives and praying for the sick wherever and whenever prayer was needed or requested. When they opened the front door to the neighborhood hospital, it happened again. God provided what they needed at the right time and in the right place.

They had arrived at the neighborhood hospital to visit two different relatives: Dad's niece Petra and Mom's nephew Osvaldo, who both were patients. Dad's niece was the first person on his mind. He intended to ask for her by name at the reception desk but thought he would have trouble locating her, as he only had a partial name. He knew that as a Mexican, she would have two or three names following her first name. Her last name was easy to remember because it was the same as his: Rivera.

However, they did not end up visiting Petra first. After they opened the front door, they saw Mom's niece Maye walking toward them. Her husband, Osvaldo, was gravely ill and was in a special unit of the hospital.

Maye greeted them warmly, hugged my mom, and said, "Osvaldo esta muy malo." Switching to English, she took a breath and translated, "He's very sick. Very, very sick."

Dad doesn't identify Osvaldo's illness in his recordings, but the doctors had informed the family that he was not going to live much longer. Maye said that his room was on the fifth floor, where an attendant would ask them to wear protective masks, which would not hinder their ability to speak or be heard during their visit. Then she asked if Dad and Mom would be praying for Osvaldo. Dad assured her that he would.

When their masks were in place, they entered the room. Dad tells us the situation was scary, as Osvaldo was visibly shaking. The seriousness of his illness was clearly evident in that special room.

My parents greeted Osvaldo and met his mother, Geneva, who was vigilantly standing on the opposite side of the hospital bed, attending to her son. After asking him how he was feeling, Dad continued by saying, "The Lord sent me here so that I can pray for you. He is going heal you, but you have got to give your heart to Jesus. You have to ask Jesus to forgive your sins."

As Osvaldo's mother listened intently while Dad talked to her son about Jesus, he noticed tears forming in the corners of her eyes.

Dad continued his message. "Why don't you give your heart to Jesus, Osvaldo? Do you want me to pray for you so that you can surrender and give your heart to Jesus?"

There was no answer from the gravely ill young man, who continued to shake as he lay on his deathbed. When no answer was forthcoming from him, Dad turned his head and saw tears rolling down Geneva's cheeks.

He asked her, "Why are you crying?"

"Well," she said, "you asked my son to confess to Jesus. He doesn't want to, but I want to confess to Jesus."

Consequently, there at the bedside of her dying son, Dad guided Geneva through prayer as she confessed her sins and asked Jesus to come into her heart.

Before leaving the room, Dad prayed for Osvaldo as well, and he left him with these words: "The Lord is going to heal you from this illness. And remember that somehow, somewhere, a little later on, you are gonna have to surrender to Jesus."

Dad goes on to tell us that Osvaldo had hardened his heart. Dad knew firsthand that nonbelievers were difficult to reach when it came to matters of Jesus Christ. Dad knew that scenario well, as he had grown up in the Catholic faith, and when God had sent a family friend to deliver a message from God to him, he had rejected the message that day. It wasn't until twenty-seven years later that Dad confessed his sins to Jesus and his life changed forever.

Dad tells us that when he prayed for the young man, the Spirit of the Lord was there and touched him, and he eventually was released from the hospital. Dad unwittingly became an agent of change in Geneva's life as she repented of her sins. I believe that Dad's words have been forever written on Osvaldo's heart and that his destiny changed. The years will pass, and the words exchanged that day in the hospital will be remembered in both of their hearts.

My parents did not locate Dad's niece Petra that day. Instead, they found Mom's niece Maye as they entered the main doors of the medical center, and they were sent to visit Osvaldo. Osvaldo received healing, and his mother made the decision to give her heart to Jesus.

A cousin told me that Osvaldo is living a normal, healthy life today but is no longer married to Maye. Occasionally, my cousin sees Geneva while out grocery shopping. They greet each other politely in passing, and just like the shopping carts they use, life rolls on by between them. It is my strong belief that God's words are never wasted. I firmly believe that Osvaldo can recall every word of the prayer Dad said that day. That prayer is imprinted on his soul. One day God will make a way for the same words to come back to his heart. He will have another chance to have his life altered if he decides to confess his sins and ask Jesus to come into his heart, just as his mother did.

As I watch the new TV series *God Friended Me*, I believe that Dad was a man who was ahead of his time, and I believe the stories he left us would be insightful to the creators, Steven Lilien and Bryan Wynbrandt, along with the executive producers, Greg Berlanti and Marcos Siega. These men have cleverly and insightfully regulated humor and drama to bring us uplifting stories that teach us how God is in control of our destinies.

Dad didn't have to make up the stories he left us on cassette tape. His stories are as indisputable today as the day they happened. Apparently, stories like his are entertaining a targeted audience, and the episodes remind us that God's words and deeds, guided into the right time and right place, are never wasted.

"Thank You, Jesus! Hallelujah!"

> *Tell your sins to each other. And pray for each other so you may be healed. The prayer from the heart of a man right with God has much power.* (**James 5:16 NLV**)

CHAPTER 11

We Gonna Need to Pray for This Flight

A severe snowstorm with icy conditions was affecting the entire Midwest area of the country as Mom and Dad landed at Chicago's O'Hare International Airport. Their journey to their Ohio home had begun earlier that winter morning in Texas. As snowbirds, they often made the trip using American Airlines and had two connecting flights before landing in Ohio, where they then had a long car ride home.

That day's travel itinerary included a one-hour-and-thirty-four-minute flight on a normal-sized airliner and then a three-hour layover. The next leg lasted two hours before they arrived at Chicago's O'Hare Airport. They knew the weather would be colder on the flight home to Ohio, but they didn't expect the flight attendant's announcement just before landing at Chicago.

"Good afternoon, Ladies and Gentlemen," the flight attendant began. "We will be arriving in Chicago in twenty minutes at terminal two, gate F3. Due to weather conditions in the area, we have been advised that some departing flights have been delayed. If you are continuing to another destination, please check the departure monitors for flight information. Thank you for choosing American Airlines. We look forward to serving you again."

Dad had learned from experience that Chicago was going to be cold, and he was quick to tell friends not to travel there at all during the wintertime. "Man, I tell you: do not go to Chicago in the wintertime! It is cold there!" he would exclaim.

The flights so far that day had been on comfortable, normal-sized

Boeing 737 aircraft. As Dad tells us, trips on smaller airplanes prompted lots of praying and soul searching. When they landed in Chicago, their hopes of having a short flight home were about to change.

Dad liked to tell people that his wife was a nice lady, but when she wanted to do something, she wanted to do it now. Getting upset easily was one of the new symptoms she exhibited as she progressed from mild to moderate dementia. Dad noted her distress, even though the flight attendant who had made the announcement about possible delays had smiled at Mom sweetly and had kind words for them during their time on board the airplane that day. Mom was not happy with the regulation-attired lady, who was only doing her job when she delivered the discouraging news that might prolong the trip home.

After they deplaned, the information monitor they had been advised to check informed them that their last flight into Ohio had been canceled. The terminal was a sea of luggage of all shapes and sizes. It seemed that every inch of flooring was covered with people using their duffel bags or suitcases as pillows; stranded passengers contorted their bodies into various configurations in an effort to find comfort as flight cancellations became an unwelcome reality.

Mom showed Dad how unhappy she was by saying, "Oh, Rianco, I want to go home. I wanna go home right now!"

To reassure her that leaving O'Hare was seemingly impossible, Dad suggested she look at all the people lying on the floor and trying to sleep in the chairs, and he explained that the people were not there by choice. They were there because their flights had been canceled, and getting a flight to Ohio would be a hard task accomplish, he told her as gently as he could.

Mom was not having anything to do with his explanation, "You start looking for a flight so we can go home tonight. I don't want to stay here with these people any longer!" Mom replied stubbornly.

At that point, Dad knew his fate was sealed. He had to at least show Mom he would try to get her home by asking the ticketing agent at the nearest gate for flight possibilities. When Dad was insistent on finding a flight out of Chicago that night, the man said, "Sir, why do you want to leave Chicago tonight during this bad weather? You see all these people? They are waiting here because none of the planes are able to leave because of the storm."

Dad persisted with his plea by telling the agent that his wife was feeling a little sick and wanted to go home that night.

"Well," the ticket agent said, "if you really want to go to Ohio tonight, there might be a way."

The agent instructed Dad to take the escalator down to the first floor, exit the terminal building, and look for the little green bus marked "Milwaukee Airport." They were to get on that shuttle, which would take them to another building where there might be a small plane heading to Ohio. The agent instructed them to make sure they sat in the front seat of the shuttle so that upon arrival, they would be the first people in line at the ticket office.

That was what they did. They weren't alone on the shuttle when it arrived at its destination, and they made sure they were the first passengers at the desk and paid for their tickets. Sixteen other people were eager to fly to Ohio that winter evening as well.

The airplane was apparently a small commuter plane, the kind with one seat on one side of the narrow aisle and two seats on the other to the back of the cabin. Mom and Dad chose the front seats and got as comfortable as possible on the small aircraft. They had plenty of time to watch their fellow travelers board and couldn't help but notice the last passenger to board the tiny airplane. She had a difficult time getting to the last empty seat at the rear of the plane because the aisles were narrow and, as Dad tells us, she was a big lady.

As if making fun of herself by admitting that her size might affect the weight and balance components of takeoff and landing, Dad tells us she surprised everyone by saying, "We gonna need to pray for this flight!"

"Amen, sister!" Dad said.

She replied, "We have got to pray now!"

"Yeah, we gonna pray," Dad announced in his broken English. Then, as he bowed his head and began to pray aloud, the others in the little cabin joined him by closing their eyes and bowing their heads respectfully or prayerfully as well.

Soon the uniformed pilot appeared at the front of the cabin and informed them that he could not guarantee he would be able to complete the flight, but he was willing to make an effort. He said, "If the Lord wants us to go, we will go. Once I start the engines, I will let them warm up for a few minutes before takeoff. I'll fly low around the city three times to continue monitoring how the engines are warming. If the engine gauges do not show adequate warming, I'll land the airplane here at this airport, because without a warm engine, we will never make the flight to Ohio."

Dad tells us that the Lord was with them again that night, as the trip was successful. He was a firm believer in the power of prayer and how it could be answered anytime during any given situation. The trip took longer than expected, as travel in the air was slower due to the weather conditions. Their normal two-hour-and-sixteen-minute trip had been extended to almost four hours. I imagine Mom was happy to be able to sleep in her own bed that night. I'm sure Dad was even happier that he and Mom didn't have to spend the night at the Chicago airport.

Dad attempts to stop the recording session with his normal "Thank You, Jesus!" It seems he was still intent on prayer as he reached to push the Stop button on the tape recorder, as he adds a few extra words to remind us about the prayer request from the last passenger to board American Airlines flight 1026 on that windy, cold winter night.

His voice rings out loud and clear before he stops speaking into the tape recorder: "But I praise the Lord! He brought us home safely that night. In the name of Jesus, I pray, Lord. Thank You, Jesus."

I imagine that Mom quietly added, "Yes, I thank You, Jesus, for my husband, who was able to find a flight home tonight."

We are sure that if we ask anything that He wants us to have,
He will hear us. **(1 John 5:14 NLV)**

CHAPTER 12

It Looked Like We Was Gonna Be with Jesus

Three of the fourteen stories Dad left us on cassette tape were about situations that happened during airplane flights. This trip is a perfect example of how prayer and faith work hand in hand to ensure safe air travel—but not necessarily without the predictable element of fear.

As I said, my parents were so-called snowbirds who traveled south to spend the winter season in Texas. The next flight I will describe took place during a particularly bad snowstorm. Once again, their trip began in Texas, and then they had a stop in Chicago's O'Hare Airport before the last leg into Ohio.

My parents probably boarded a Boeing 737 for the first leg of the flight. Dad is quick to let us know that all of the aircraft they boarded during the trip were bigger planes, as opposed to smaller propeller or commuter aircraft. This fact is an important component because several experiences that frightened them happened while they were aboard smaller commuter-type aircraft. Having to fly in a smaller plane added the factor of fear to the flight, due of the size of the plane. The fear factor in this adventure was not the size of the airplane, because Dad doesn't mention flying in a small aircraft. Instead, inclement weather was the cause of distress.

There was a snowstorm affecting flight visibility for the pilot and crew; therefore, the flight involved filing a mandated flight plan using instrument flight rules (IFR), as required by the Federal Aviation Administration (FAA).

Even though they boarded a large airliner for the flight, the cabin was relatively empty. The captain informed the passengers and crew that they would attempt to make the trip even though the weather was marginal. He explained that visibility was poor, and he would be flying under special flight rules with all the proper flight instruments necessary to make the trip safely. Furthermore, the pilot said the passengers would understand more about the poor visibility once the plane was in the air.

On the tape recording, Dad is animated as he says that if you have never been scared during an airplane flight, you will learn all about being scared if you have to fly during bad weather. There are a lot of scary situations out there in the aviation world, he informs us.

On that particular flight, on that large aircraft, there were about forty people on board. The attendants, who were dressed for cold weather in slacks and sweater vests, instructed each person where to sit, giving out specific seat assignments in order to conform to weight and balance requirements for the plane to operate safely. That day, Mom and Dad were not sitting side by side, as was their customary routine. Passengers had been instructed to leave one seat empty between them.

The front and middle sections of the main cabin were empty, according to the specific requirements. The captain, cocaptain, and flight attendants were the only persons located at the front of the plane.

Once the airplane was in the air, due to turbulence caused by flying through the clouds, the plane started shaking, leaving passengers with the feeling that it was going to break apart while maintaining speed and gaining altitude. It was a scary situation for almost everyone, not just Dad and Mom. Dad admits that he was exceptionally frightened.

Dad tells us that the man sitting across the aisle to his left was playing a game on his computer, which, to Dad, was an indication that the man was not scared at all.

All of a sudden, the plane shook more violently. Dad started to holler because the sensation was more terrifying. "It looked like we was gonna be with Jesus!" he tells us.

When the man sitting across the aisle heard the terror in Dad's voice, he offered to switch seats with Mom so they could sit closer together, hoping that would make them feel more comfortable. However, it didn't help much. As Dad says, "We were scared, man! I tell you that!"

The pilot announced how turbulent the flight was going to be because of the snow and wind. He said in the way of comfort, "But with the help of the Lord, we are going to try to make this flight safely."

Landing in Ohio proved to be a scary ordeal because the snow and wind were still blowing hard. At the end of the telling, Dad joyfully announces, "The Lord came through again!" They landed safely.

Dad gives praise to the Lord for the safe trip and reminds us that Jesus promised never to leave us alone and never forsake us. Even though the flight invoked fear in the hearts of my parents, I believe their hearts were right with their Maker. Their faith in Jesus Christ is what amplifies this simple yet powerful featured memory. They were both great role models for not only their nine offspring but also the twenty-two grandchildren and fifty-eight great- grandchildren God blessed them with. Our parents did their best to live lives that honored Jesus Christ. What a legacy they left us!

Once again, Dad ends by humbling himself in prayer and saying, "In the name of Jesus, I pray. Amen. Hallelujah!"

> *And my tongue will tell about how right and good You are, and about Your praise all day long.* **(Psalm 35:28 NLV)**

CHAPTER 13

I Want a Big Plane—How Much?

This last aviation anecdote took place in the state of Washington, which has been home to one of my uncles and his family for as long as I can remember. This might have been the last flight my parents took aboard a small aircraft. They flew from Ohio to Washington to spend time with my mother's brother, who was living his last days on earth. After living a life full of great memories, my uncle passed away during that visit at the age of seventy-six. His father had lived a full seventy-nine years, and his mother had lived a full life of eighty-one years. My mother passed away five years after her brother, also having lived a full life surpassing seventy years.

Prior to this retelling, I spoke to one of my uncle's daughters, who graciously shared her memories of this visit but wished to remain anonymous.

I first categorized this memory as an aviation theme, but after I spoke to my cousin, I am convinced that it speaks more about living life in such a manner that when you leave this earth, people will be able to say that you lived life to the fullest. Is it a coincidence that as I prepared this part of the manuscript, someone reminded me to, "live life to **live** it"?

The state of Washington is in the Northwest region of the United States, where the Cascade Mountain range—a major mountain range of western North America—extends south from Canada's British Columbia through Washington and Oregon into Northern California. It includes Mount Rainer, which has a stately lodge that my cousin takes all her visitors to see during their once-in-a-lifetime trips to Washington.

Before landing at Yakima Air Terminal Airport-McAllister Field (YKM), you have to fly into Seattle-Tacoma International Airport (SEA), also known to the locals as SeaTac. Mom and Dad flew into SEA airport on a major airline, or "a big plane," as Dad says. Dad tells us that he became frightened during the next leg of their trip on a small commuter plane when he could hear air coming into the cabin from underneath the door at the rear of the plane. He says, "The little plane made a noise like *ca-cha*, *ca-cha*, *ca-cha*, *ca-cha*, *ca-cha*. It sounded like it was going to break down."

The trip from SEA to YKM included airtime through various mountain ranges. I don't know which mountain Dad talks about during the recording, but as the flight approached YKM, it included a view of Mount Rainer in the background at 14,411 feet. Yakima County's Cleman Mountain ridge, which surrounds the Yakima Valley, has an elevation of 4,195 feet, so the passengers would have been able to see both mountain ranges.

I love Dad's description of the view in his broken English, as follows:

> But that mountain! I don't know how high the mountain was. But the mountains were tall mountains. First, we had to fly toward the *big* mountain. After you get to the mountain, you have to go down into a valley. Once you go down into the valley, the airport is there. I don't know how they do it! But anyhow, I was so scared. Then I thought that the plane was gonna break down on top of the mountain, because it was making so much noise. I was frightened because the air coming through the bottom of the door from the outside at the back of the plane was very loud!

Dad and Mom went directly to the main terminal after descending the portable stairs and boldly announced their concerns to the clerk at the ticket counter. Dad said, "Madam, I want to tell you one thing. I don't want to go back to Seattle on my return trip on that little plane. I want to fly back to Seattle on a big plane! How much to fly back on a bigger plane?"

They were advised that not many big airplanes flew people into SEA, but for thirty-five dollars each, they could make the return trip on one that was a little bit bigger. Dad agreed to pay the extra fare, hoping the plane would not shake all over.

My cousin explained that during my parents' visit in Washington, they spent the daytime hours visiting places of interest. The vistas from the Yakima Valley included old barns beside orchards and fields and a road that led to a stately lodge up the mountainside. The uphill approach to Mount Rainer Lodge steepened and narrowed, causing passengers sitting by the door to nervously inch closer to the center of the vehicle. The trade-off for narrow roads and steep drop-offs was the breathtaking view.

They spent the evening hours sitting in their living room, surrounding my uncle's hospital bed, making memories and letting life happen. They shared stories, recalled events, laughed, cried, and sang old beloved songs, such as "The Old Rugged Cross" and "Amazing Grace." They made sure they helped my uncle live the last days of his life on earth to the fullest there in the beautiful Yakima Valley in the state of Washington.

When I spoke to my cousin, she shared an amazing thought and private moment she had one morning as she thanked God for her life and the surroundings He had given her. She gave me permission to include it here.

One morning, she sat in her living room, looking out the window, thanking God for giving her the beautiful view of the Cascade Mountains and the mighty Columbia River to look at every morning. "You didn't have to give this view to me, but you did," she said, in awe of the beauty before her. "This must be your greatest creation!'" she humbly added as she spoke to God.

Instantly, a voice came back to her: "No, **you** are my greatest creation!"

She interpreted the word *you* as referring to *all* humans. Humans are God's greatest creation.

This anecdote isn't limited to flying experiences. It reminds us to live life to its fullest, which is one explanation for why God created us. Maybe living life to its fullest means flying above Mount Rainer or landing in a small airplane in the Yakima Valley with the Columbia River flowing freely southbound. Maybe it means being at the bedside of a loved one who is making a journey into the next life. Or perhaps it's all about having a conversation with someone that you didn't know you should have had. It could also mean remembering to give someone a smile when you notice that he or she isn't wearing one. Above all, life is what you make it. Be kind to someone today simply because.

Dad finishes the session with these words: "I praise the Lord because He helped us as we traveled to visit my brother-in-law during his last days on earth. The Lord promised that He would be with us until the end of time. Oh, hallelujah! I praise the Lord for that!"

Then he adds, "I wanna sing a little chorus before it gets too late." That chorus follows:

> There's a river of life flowing out of me. Made the lame
> to walk and the blind to see. Opened precious doors, set
> the captives free. There's a river of life flowing out of me![3]

After this reading, I hope that you experience a river of life flowing out of you. You don't have to stand tall like Mount Rainer in the Cascade Mountain range with the mighty Columbia River carving out a valley at your feet. Begin small. Give someone a smile, and begin to live life to *live* it!

"Thank You, Jesus! Hallelujah!"

The Lord—Our Shepherd

The Lord is my Shepherd. I will have everything I need. He lets me rest in fields of green grass. He leads me beside the quiet waters. He makes me strong again. He leads me in the way of living right with Himself which brings honor to His name. Yes, even if I walk through the valley of the shadow of death, I will not be afraid of anything, because You are with me. You have a walking stick with which to guide and one with which to help. These comfort me. You are making a table of food ready for me in front of those who hate me. You have poured oil on my head. I have everything I need. For sure, You will give me goodness and loving-kindness all the days of my life. Then I will live with You in Your house forever. **(Psalm 23 NLV)**

[3] Betty Carr Pulkingham, L. Caseboldt, and Kaitlyn Scott, "I've Got a River of Life," 1971, 1975, http://www.higherpraise.com/Lyrics4/RiverOfLife.htm.

CHAPTER 14

Keep Talking about Jesus

As I listened to this section of Dad's tape recordings, it was clear he intended this to be his last entry. He begins by telling his sisters in Christ who encouraged him to begin the project that he will finish the recordings that day. He finishes the recording session, but then he adds, "I'll just keep talking about Jesus!" By the time he finishes talking, he has recorded fourteen stories. There are so many stories to tell that he "could talk all day and night," he says before he ends this session. But once again, God had other plans.

He begins this would-be last session by saying, "Sisters, today is Saturday, the third day of July, and I have come back to tape record the rest of my testimonial. Like I have told you before, I had felt so lost in my life. I didn't know anything about the Lord. But today, with Jesus, I have a lot of things that keep me living. And today I will finish telling you my testimonial."

One of the greatest legacies Dad left for us is this collection of stories. By reading the words of this simple man, complete with his broken English and poor grammar, we learn how God changed his troubled soul and gave him a tender, grateful heart. While Dad was recording these stories, some days he seemed distracted, but he never forgot his audience and his mission to tell people about his life with Jesus, because the Lord had been good to him and had changed his life for the better.

He didn't tire of telling people how to surrender to the call of Christ by kneeling down and confessing their sins. He offered them a simple prayer to repeat: "Lord, forgive my sins. I want you to make me whole. I want you to change me. I want to live for you, Jesus."

Some of his recorded sessions contain short messages, because he believed he had a vital and true message for people to listen to. The Lord had given him a good memory, along with wisdom and understanding. Dad continued to walk for Him in the best way he knew how on a day-to-day basis. Every day he yearned to live for Christ and grew closer to Him.

Dad knew in his heart that Jesus would return to earth one day, and he also knew that the Lord was still in the business of saving lives. After all, Christ died on the cross to pay the price for the sins of mankind.

Even a month before Dad died, he was giving thanks for little things others did for him. Every time I brought him a glass of water to quench his thirst, he tenderly, kindly, and gratefully said, "Thank you. Thank you." If he was lying in bed and someone fluffed his pillow, he remembered to thank him or her.

Three weeks before Dad passed away at the age of nearly ninety years, I sat with him as his weakened body prepared itself to separate from its soul. One nurse, while keeping vigil, would softly sing songs for him to hear, believing that hearing would be the last of his five senses to leave his body before he began his journey into the next life. One day, as that nurse adjusted the quilt over his shoulders, she remarked that he was taking his time with the transition. Then she quietly left us alone in the room appointed with his wheelchair; his favorite snack of pistachio nuts; clean plaid pajamas; and my stack of neatly folded bedding, clothing, and puzzle books I had brought with me to help pass the seemingly endless days.

That same day, I heard the telltale sound of footsteps echo in the hall outside Dad's room, indicating family members were gathering in small groups to exchange long hugs, shed tears of pain, and exchange heartfelt condolences upon having received news that their loved one had made their transition. Guilt, inner shame, and embarrassment filled my heart when I realized that my first thought, although I did not voice it, was *That family is lucky. They get to go home now.*

The next time I recognized the familiar signs that someone was probably in transition, instead of letting that selfish thought enter my head again, I picked up a puzzle book to occupy my time after checking to see if Dad needed his pillow fluffed or his ice refreshed, and I took time to give thanks for the precious gift of time I had been given in his presence. One sister told me several times that the hours she spent with him were long and tiresome, but she got much more from the experience than she put into it. As it turns out, Ramona's remarks were right on point.

An hour later, his skin seemed to turn grayer, there was a dullness in his skin tone, and his arms and fingers were extended away from his body as if reaching to touch some unknown thing that was not apparent to me. Then, in his weakened state, Dad opened the weary slits that were his eyes and motioned for me to come closer with a gentle movement of his head and the slow motion of his beckoning eyes as he used his whispered breath to announce what I thought would be his last words. However, he said, "Jesus said I have to stay here another little while."

His color and strength slowly returned during the next few minutes, and for the next two weeks, he remained on earth. During his last week, a sister told me that Dad had been visiting with another patient in a room down the hall, offering prayers of comfort. It was apparent that God still had work for Dad to do before He took him to heaven.

I, too, feel that there is additional work to do as I near the conclusion of transcribing and retelling the stories Dad left behind. They are amazing stories of how God changed Dad's life and directed him to impact the lives of others. Even though he was a simple man, his faith could move mountains.

If you are reading this, Dad is continuing to talk about Jesus in the form of a printed script. Dad never tired of telling us that Jesus is the only one who can save the soul of a man, woman, boy, girl, young man, or old man. And He can do it anytime, he would say.

I would be remiss if I did not leave you with the parting words on the cassette tape:

> He's got the power. He died for us on the cross. He paid that price for us because He wanted to make us free. The Lord is real! Anytime you ask Him something, He can do it!
>
> I believe that you can ask something and He can answer your prayers. He can! He can answer prayers!

And then somehow, somewhere, when we obey, we know that we are in good hands. Jesus is the one that can save us. Jesus is the one that can tell us which way to go, either this way or that way.

I can imagine the last moments of his tape-recording session: Seated outdoors under the shade tree of his family home, with his tape recorder on his lap and his finger poised on the Stop button, he was fully confident in his ability to tell simple stories. He had recorded the short stories with his grateful heart and delivered them with the conviction of his strong faith. His work was finished. The recording sessions chronicling how God had used his prayer life to impact others had come to the end of the final chapter—but the book had not yet been completed. There was a gentle nudge on his finger as he readied to push the Stop button for the final time. His heart skipped a beat as a knowing sensation in his body was quickened by the Holy Spirit. At that moment, he knew that somehow, someway, his wish for people to read about the evidence of God's favor in his life would result in your reading his book.

"Why not?" he asked himself with a *wink* of his left eye to no one but the tape recorder.

Then came one last reminder and exclamation, "The Lord is good! Hallelujah! Thank You, Jesus!"

> You are not ever given a wish without also being given the power to make it true.
> —Richard Bach

We thank God for the hope that is being kept for you in heaven. You first heard about this hope through the Good News which is the Word of Truth. The Good News came to you the same as it is now going out to all the world. Lives are being changed, just as your life was changed the day you heard the Good News. You understood the truth about God's loving-kindness. **(Colossians 1:5–6 NLV)**

List of Scriptural Citations

Isaiah 55:11
I Peter 2:9
Matthew 18:19-20
Hebrews 13:5
2 Corinthians 12:2-3
2 Corinthians 5:17
Exodus 20:12
John 15:7
Psalms 91:9-12
James 5:15
James 5:16
I John 5:14
Psalms 35:28
Psalms 23
Collossians 1:5-6

ABOUT THE AUTHOR

The cassette recording her father made was presented to her on the day of his funeral. The first-time author transcribed his Tex-Mex English, unveiling God's plan for his prayer life and the undeniable results. Inspiration awaits the reader in this skillful blend of a father's words and his daughter's insights as she fulfills his wish to have his short stories published to glorify God.

You can reach Reyna Rivera at thetaperecorder@yahoo.com.